TRIANGLE▼POSTALS

**Human towers**
# Castells
Touching the sky with the hand   JOSEP ALMIRALL

Photography by
FÈLIX MIRÓ
XAVIER SAUMELL
CARLES CASTRO
HANS HANSEN
EDUARD GIL
MAITE GOMÀ

# Welcome to *casteller* world!

## Strength, balance, bravery and good sense

The *castells* are an exercise in special cooperation, almost unique in the world, that set about achieving ephemeral challenges, but which impregnate the photographic memory that we all conserve. Welcome to a spectacular, fantastic, unimaginable and, therefore, surprising dimension. Men and women, boys and girls, young and old, without worrying about their origins, beliefs, education, social status or reasons, who climb over each other forming apparently impossible figures, always higher, more difficult, more transcendental. They are called *castells* and the people who form them, *castellers*. They were founded in Catalonia more than two hundred years ago, and are essential in many popular festivals in this country. They thrill thousands of people, arouse passions and produce an interest equivalent to the most popular sports. Do you want to know more? Welcome to the human tower dimension.

Xiquets del Serrallo

# World Heritage

The *castells* are Intangible Cultural Heritage. UNESCO decided this on the 16 November 2010 in Nairobi, the capital of Kenya. The candidature of the *castells* to form part of this select list of traditional expressions and elements in the world to be protected was promoted from the *casteller* sphere itself, and swiftly gained the support of civil society and the Catalan institutions. The Catalan Parliament thus expressed its unanimous support and later on the Government of Spain added their support to the candidature and formalised it before UNESCO. In its evaluation, the organism of the United Nations pointed out that the *castells* are perceived by the Catalan people as an integral part of their cultural identity, passed on from generation to generation, and which provide the members of the community with a sense of continuity, social cohesion and solidarity. In this way, UNESCO recognised the universal and exceptional nature of tradition rooted in the history and identity of Catalonia. In fact, two hundred years after its beginnings, there are some sixty groups or *colles* that form *castells*, and there are more than seven thousand people who form part of them and who each year raise some sixteen thousand human constructions. The *castells* therefore, as well as being an authentic Catalan expression, have also become universal heritage. The *castells* now belong to everyone a little more.

# Summary *Castells* Touching the sky with the hand

| | |
|---|---|
| 8 | **1. Getting our bearings** |
| 9 | What do we see |
| 18 | Where and how we see it |
| 22 | Most important *diades* |
| 38 | Competition of *Castells* of Tarragona |
| 45 | The route of the *castells* |
| | |
| 46 | **2. Let's enjoy it** |
| 47 | How and from where we can see the *castells* |
| 52 | *Castells* in summer |
| 54 | Taking part in a *castell* |
| 56 | Experiencing the atmospher of the *casteller* |
| | |
| 60 | **3. The *castellers*** |
| 64 | An intergenerational world |
| 68 | The youngsters |
| 74 | The woman *castellera* |
| 78 | The kit or clothing of the *casteller* |
| 84 | Safety |

Summary

## 4. The parts of a *castell* — 88
- 90    The *pinya*
- 98    The *tronc*
- 104    The *pom de dalt*
- 108    The *folre*
- 110    The *manilles*

## 5. All the *castells* — 112
- 118    The pillar
- 132    The two, or tower
- 144    The three
- 156    The four
- 174    The five
- 186    The four with point, or pillar, in the middle
- 196    The three with point, or pillar, in the middle
- 202    The three raised from below
- 208    The castells also fall

## 6. The *diades* — 212
- 213    The rules
- 214    The value of the *castells*

## 7. The *colles* — 216
- 220    The rehearsals
- 220    The centres
- 220    The budget of the *colla*
- 222    The cost of a performance
- 222    Management of the *casteller* word

## 8. The music — 226

## 9. Two centuries building *castells* — 232

**Glossary** — 238

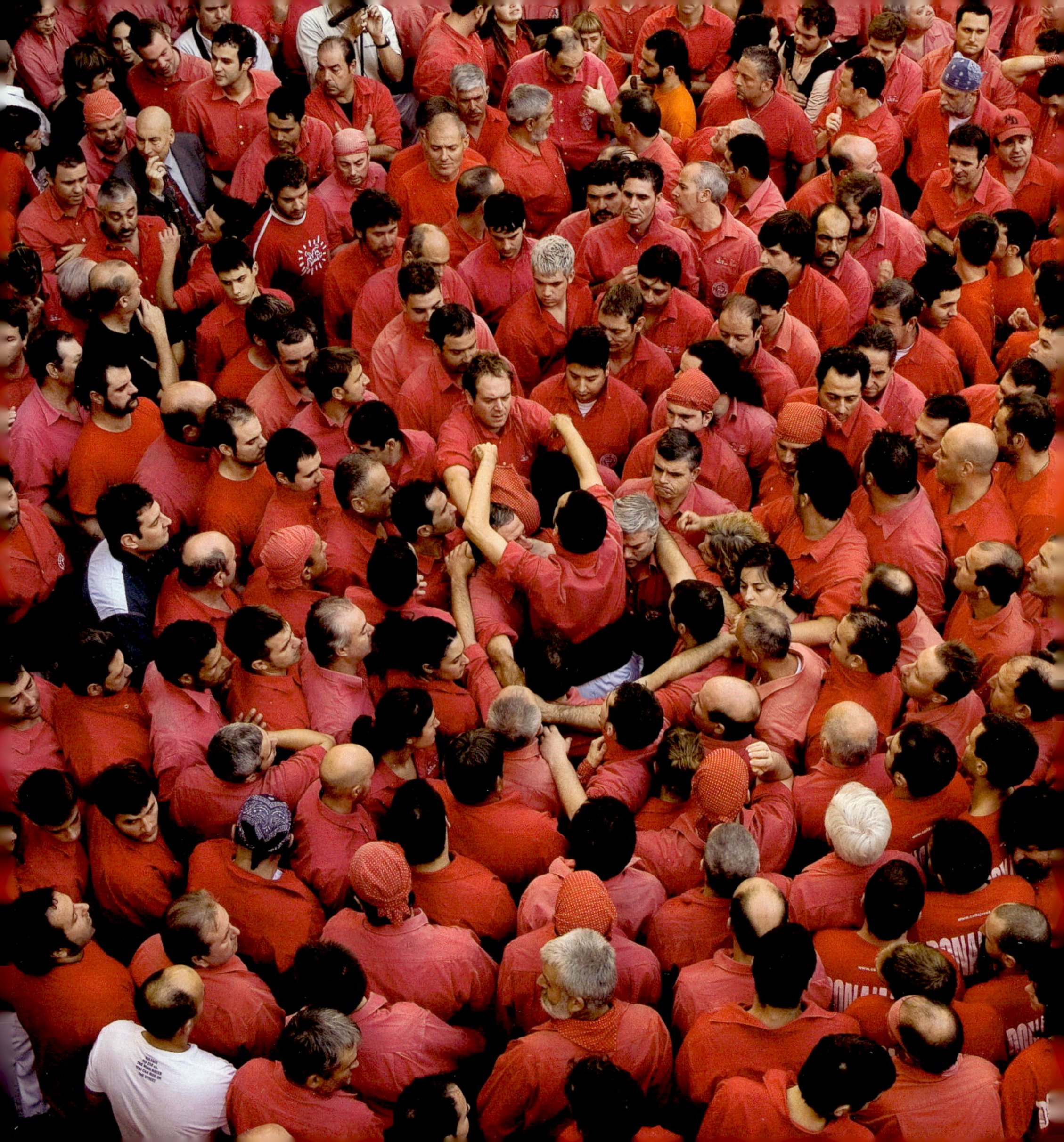

# 1. Getting our bearings

## What do we see?

Suddenly, one hundred or more people, *castellers*, press together forming a circle, a *pinya*. A *casteller*, generally their head, called *cap de colla*, gives precise instructions in Catalan and then, over the *pinya* climb a small group of *castellers*, who hold on to each other by their shoulders, while, from below, some of the *pinya* hold them by their backsides. A new group of *castellers* now climbs over those that stand out from the *pinya*. And then a group of musicians begin to play a strident tune, and more *castellers* continue climbing and making the structure grow. Now there are two small people who climb up the backs of the previous ones; they are boys and girls of around seven or eight years of age! The last one arrives to the top and raises their hand: they do the *aleta*. The tune changes dramatically. The public applaud. The *castell* has been crowned, assembled. Now they have to climb down in reverse order to the way they climbed up. When nearly all the *castellers* are on the ground, and the instruments are about to end the tune, the public applaud, the *castell* has been completed, it has disassembled, it has not *fet llenya*: it has not fallen.

The seconds of the Colla Vella dels Xiquets de Valls climbing over the *pinya*

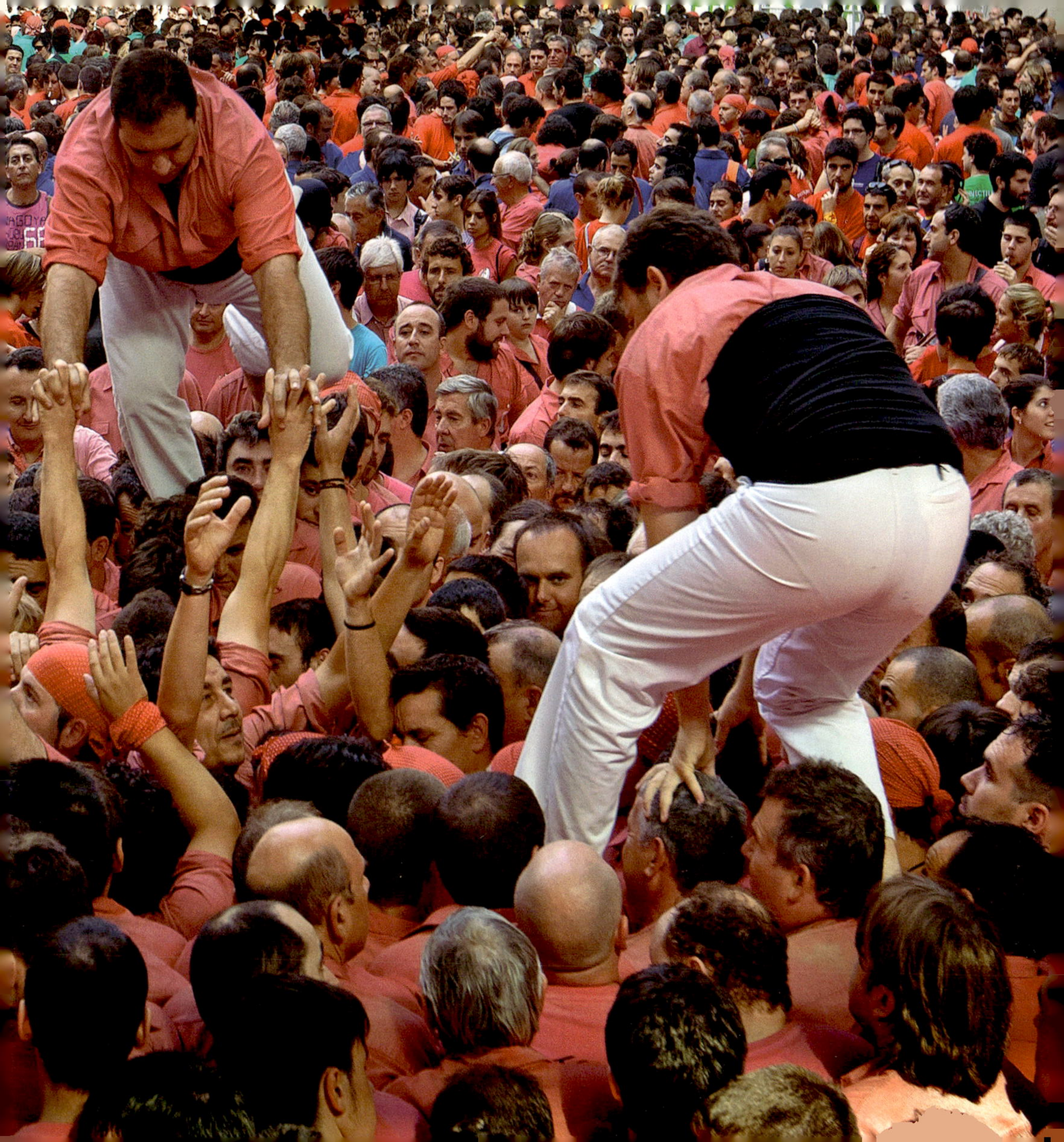

Colla Joves Xiquets de Valls

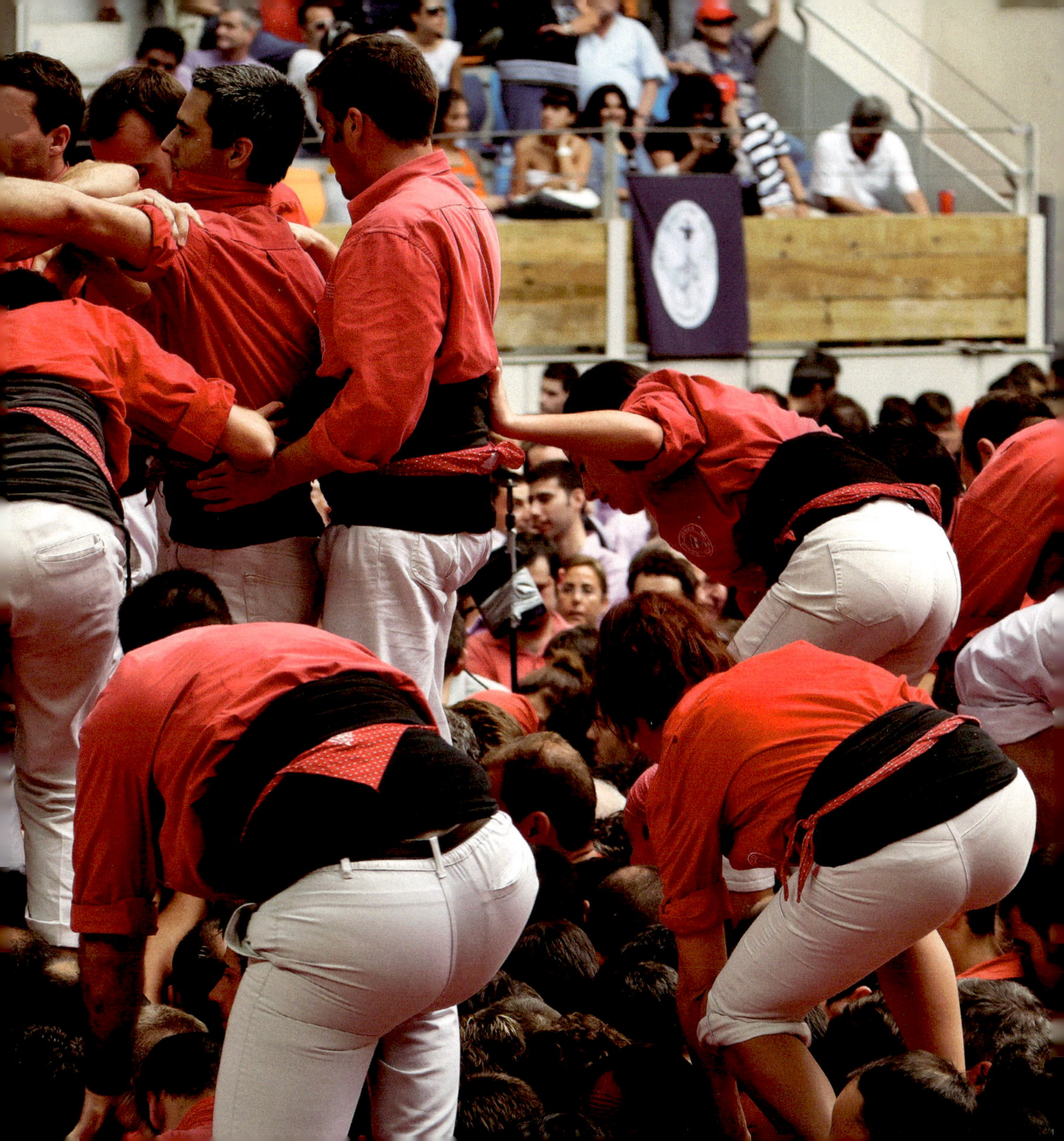

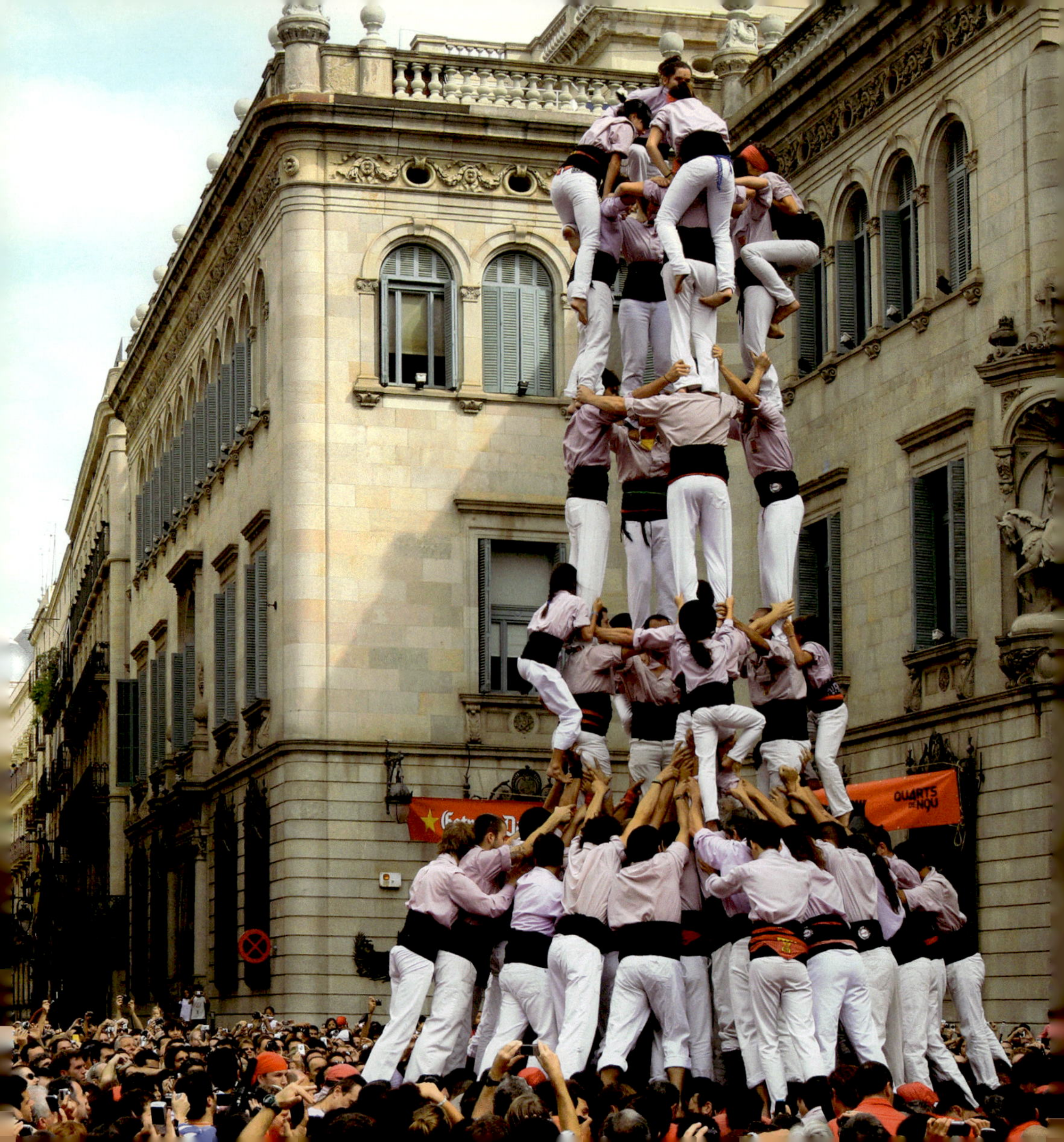
QUARTS
DE NOU

Minyons de Terrassa building the 4 of 9 with *folre*

The *enxaneta* of the Castellers de Vilafranca climbing a *pilar*

*The enxaneta of the Colla Vella dels Xiquets de Valls doing the aleta*

*The enxaneta of the Xiquets de Tarragona celebrating the success of a castell*

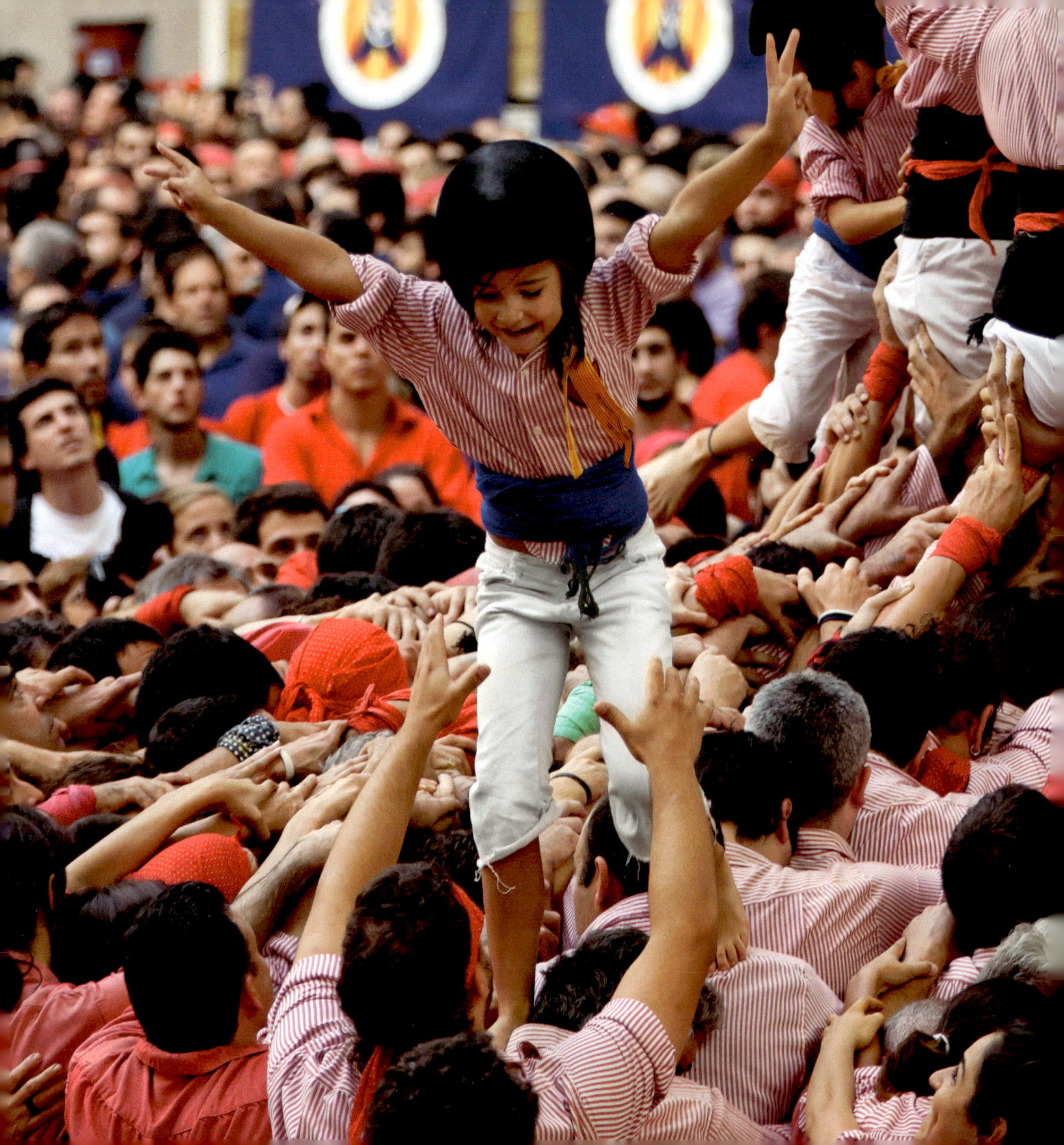

**1.** Getting our bearings

# Where and how we see it

Traditionally, the *castells* are made in the town for the town and its representatives. Therefore they are almost always in open public spaces, generally in town or city squares, often in front of the *Casa de la Vila* (the town hall building). On many occasions they are the most outstanding event and with most public at the annual festivals. Witnessing this spectacle is always free for the fans, who are capable of standing up for several hours to savour the final result of the performance of one or more *colles* of *castellers*. There are fans and *castellers* who consider that a performance or *diada castellera* is a battle between *colles* to demonstrate which is best. However, for others, it only has a meaning of self-achievement. There are also those who think that the *castells* is a sport, or a cultural act. For others it is an exercise of local or national confirmation, for others, taking part in a family tradition, for others... The fact is that they can be whatever one feels they are.

For some years now, it has been considered that the season begins around the time of Saint George's Day, the patron saint of Catalonia, on the 23 April, and ends in November. It is also true that they are made throughout the year, but it is during these eight months when a week does not pass without performances on Saturdays and Sundays. There are several media outlets in Catalonia that publish the weekly calendar of the *diades*. The *colles* announce the performances they will do on their web page. Nevertheless, the best idea is to check the web page of the CCCC, *Coordinadora de Colles Castelleres de Catalunya*, the representative body of the *castellers*. Its web address is www.cccc.cat. It shows the town, square or street, time and the *colles* that will be taking part. Another useful address is www.webcasteller.com, which also provides the road map and street map of the town. Other equally interesting addresses for consulting are www.lapinya.cat, www.lamalla.cat and www.moncasteller.cat.

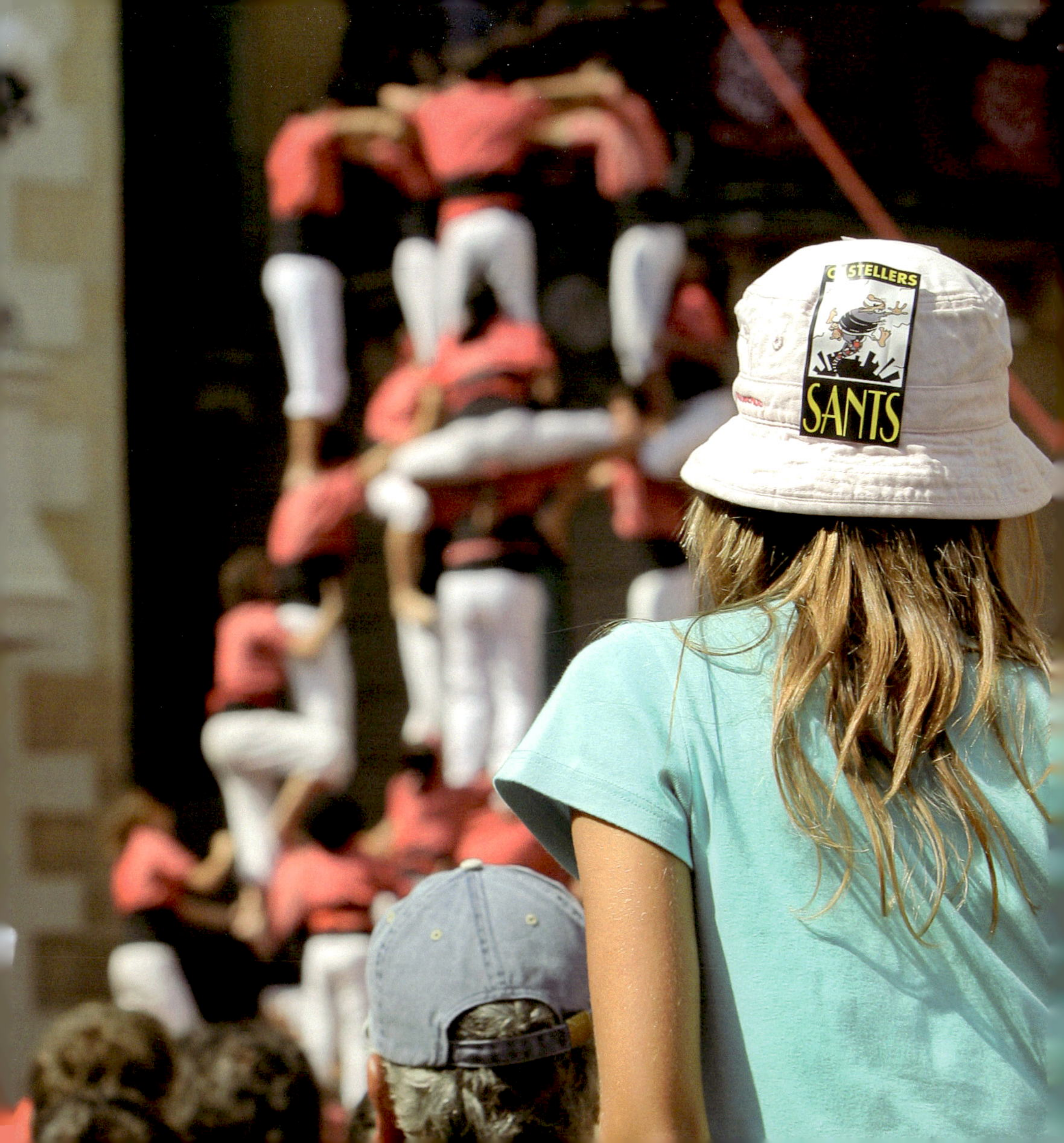
STELLERS
SANTS

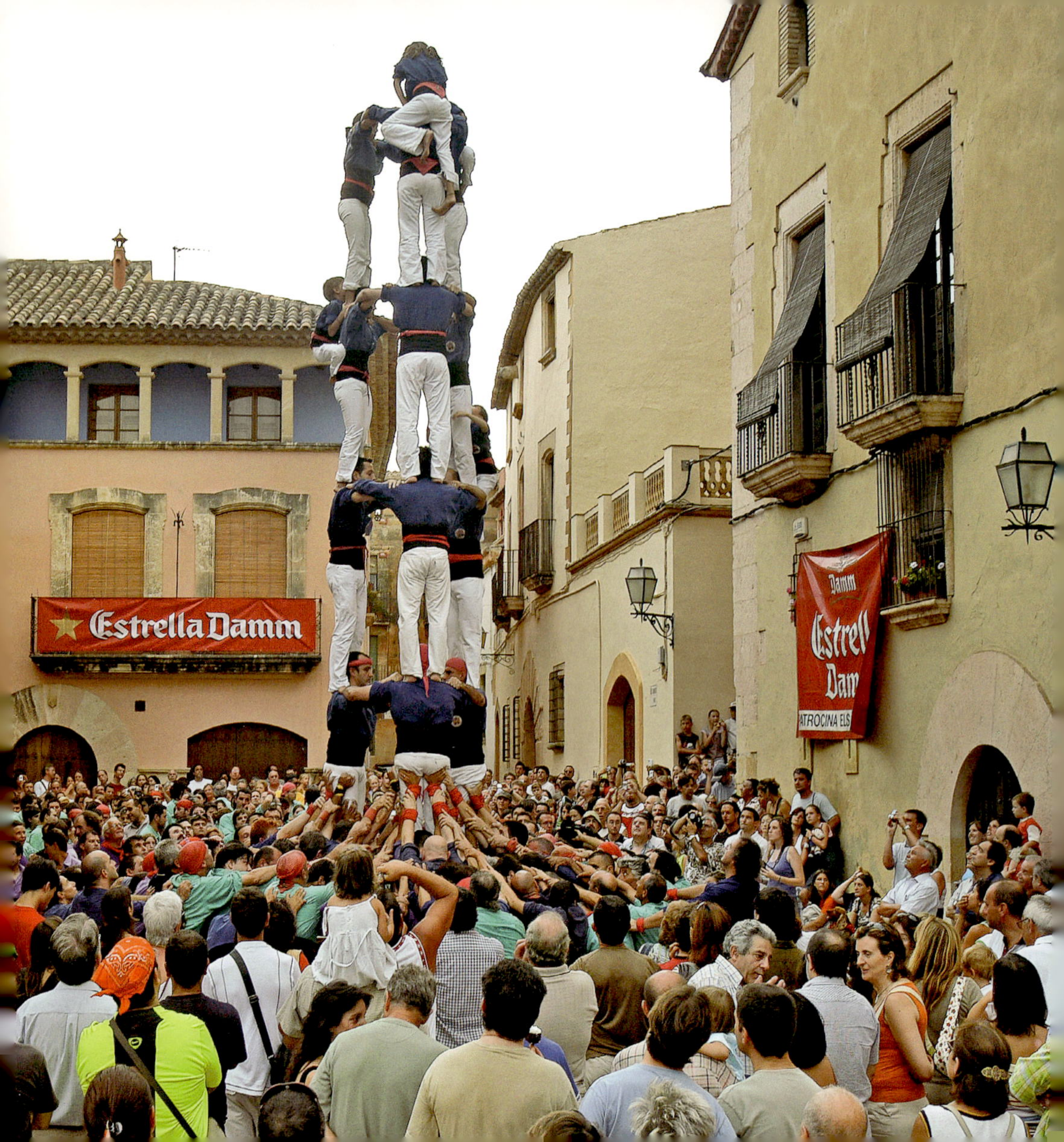
Estrella Damm
Damm
Estrell
Dam
PATROCINA ELS

Capgrossos de Mataró. Altafulla

Pillar going down steps _ Colla Jove dels Castellers de Sitges

**1.** Getting our bearings

# Most important *diades*

Every season there are hundreds of performances of *castells*, but there are a few of them that are essential for any fan. If we look at the calendar, the first big event of the year in the 24 June, on the festival of Saint John, in Valls, where the two *colles* from the city usually make the first 9-storey *castells*. On the first Sunday in July you cannot miss the performance in the Annual Festival of Terrassa where you can often see one of the most difficult *castells* formed. The last Sunday of July is another not-to-be-missed *diada,* that of Les Santes, in Mataró. August is a month with a very packed agenda. On the first Wednesday you should get to the performance of Firagost, in Valls; on the 15 in La Bisbal del Penedès, the 19 in Tarragona, at the foot of the cathedral, with all the *colles* from the city. Then the Saturday of the following week in El Catllar, a unique *castellera* square. The next day, Sunday, all eyes focus on L'Arboç, and on the 30 August, Vilafranca del Penedès, during the festivals of Saint Felix, becomes the capital of the *castells* with a performance of the four best *colles* of the moment. September plays host to two spectacular events. The first, the Annual Festival of Saint Thecla, is on the Sunday before the 23, in the Plaça de la Font in Tarragona; the other, that of the Annual Festival of the Mercè, is on the following Sunday in the Plaça Sant Jaume in Barcelona. Also in September it is wonderful to see on the 24 at midday, the four *colles* of Tarragona making a *pilar* of 4 walk five hundred metres from the cathedral to the city hall. In October, generally on the fourth Sunday, Valls once again hosts one of the more traditional days, Saint Ursula, which many years coincides with another big *diada*, that of Saint Narcissus, in Girona. The *castells* end in November with two big events. The first on the 1, All Saints Day, is in Vilafranca del Penedès, and the second, generally the third Sunday in the month, is in Terrassa.

4 of 8 with the pillar in the middle _ Colla Vella dels Xiquets de Valls. Plaça del Blat. Valls

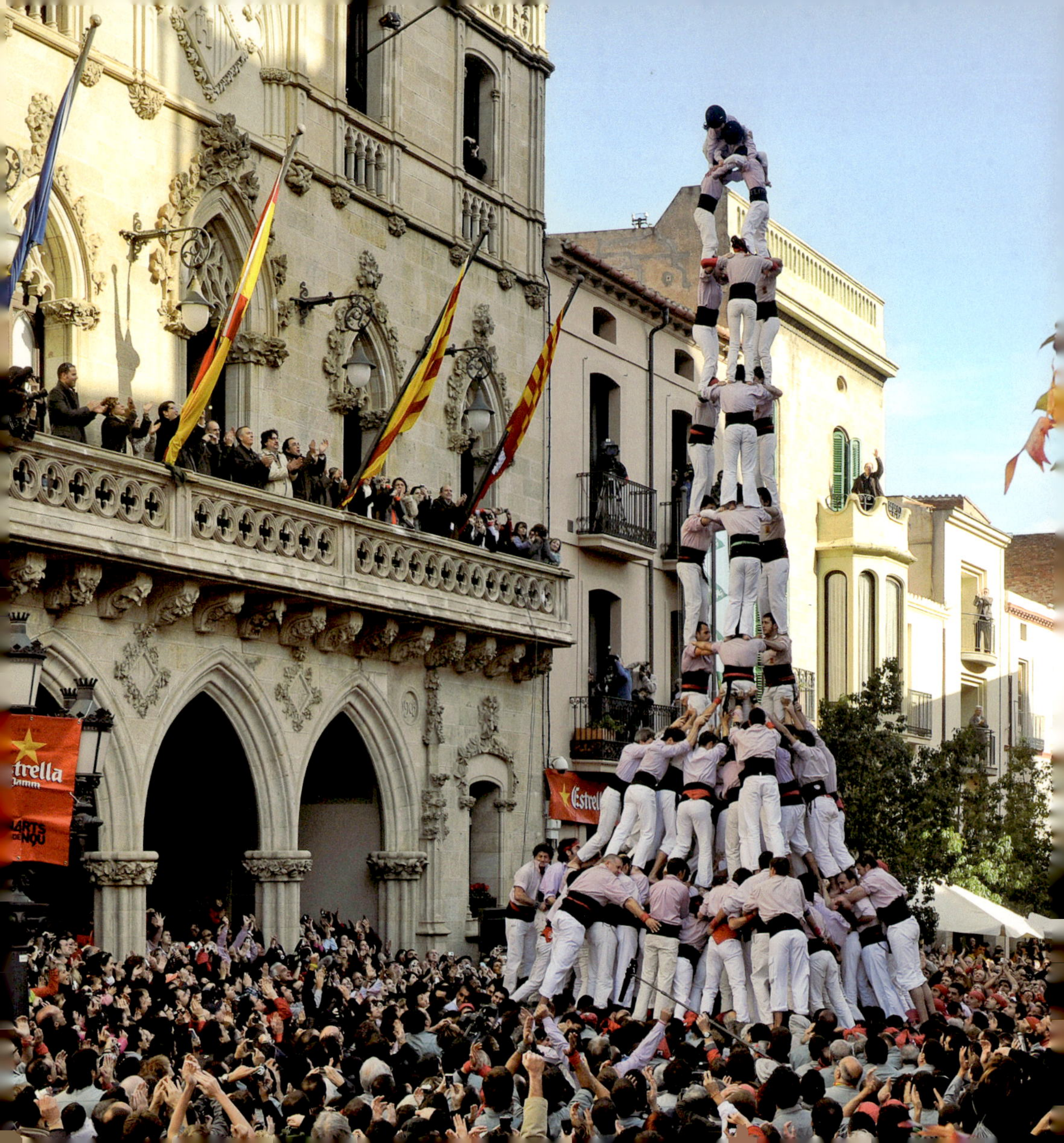

Estrella
Damm

3 of 10 with *folre* and *manilles* _ Minyons de Terrassa. Plaça del Raval de Montserrat. Terrassa

4 of 9 with *folre* _ Capgrossos de Mataró. Plaça Santa Anna. Mataró

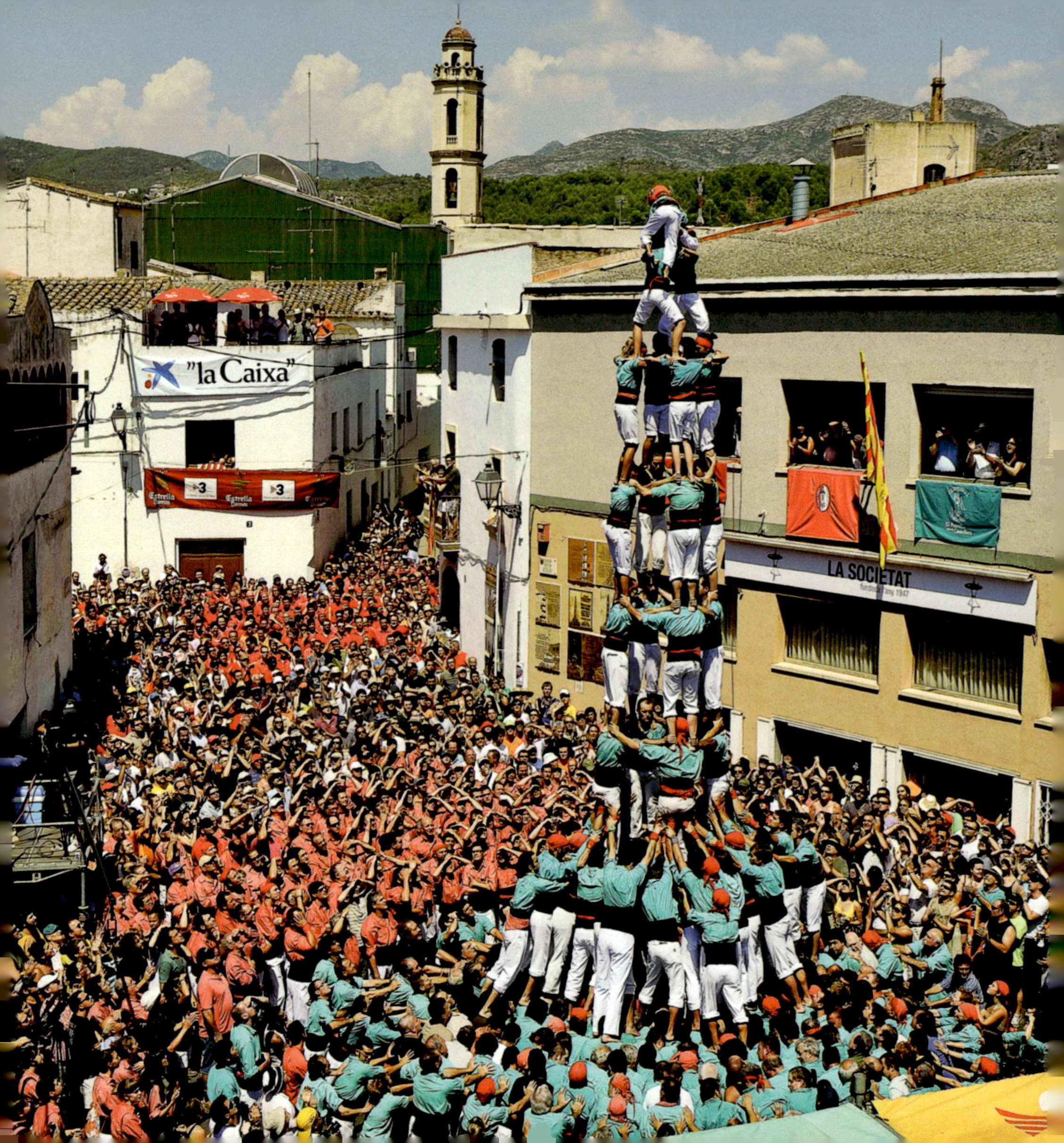
"la Caixa"
3
3
LA SOCIETAT

4 of 9 with *folre* _ Castellers de Vilafranca. La Bisbal del Penedès

3 of 9 with *folre* _ Colla Jove Xiquets de Tarragona. El Catllar

5 of 8 _ Colla Joves Xiquets de Valls. L'Arboç

5 of 9 with *folre* _ Castellers de Vilafranca. Plaça de la Vila. Vilafranca del Penedès

VEGUERIAPENEDÈS

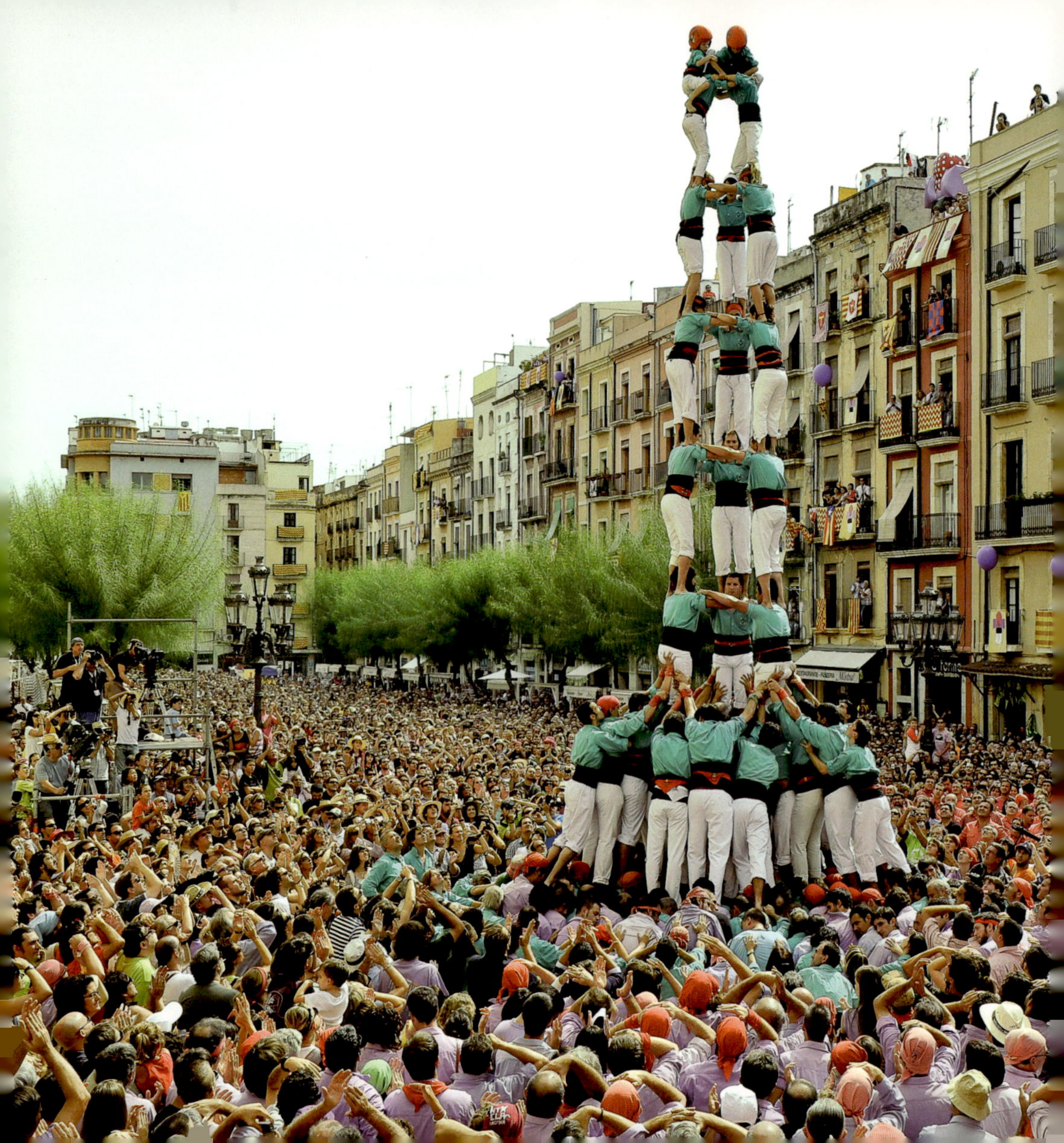

3 of 9 with *folre* _ Castellers de Vilafranca. Plaça de la Font de Tarragona

Xiquets de Tarragona going down the steps of the Cathedral of Tarragona

Castellers de Barcelona. Festivals of the Mercè. Plaça de Sant Jaume. Barcelona

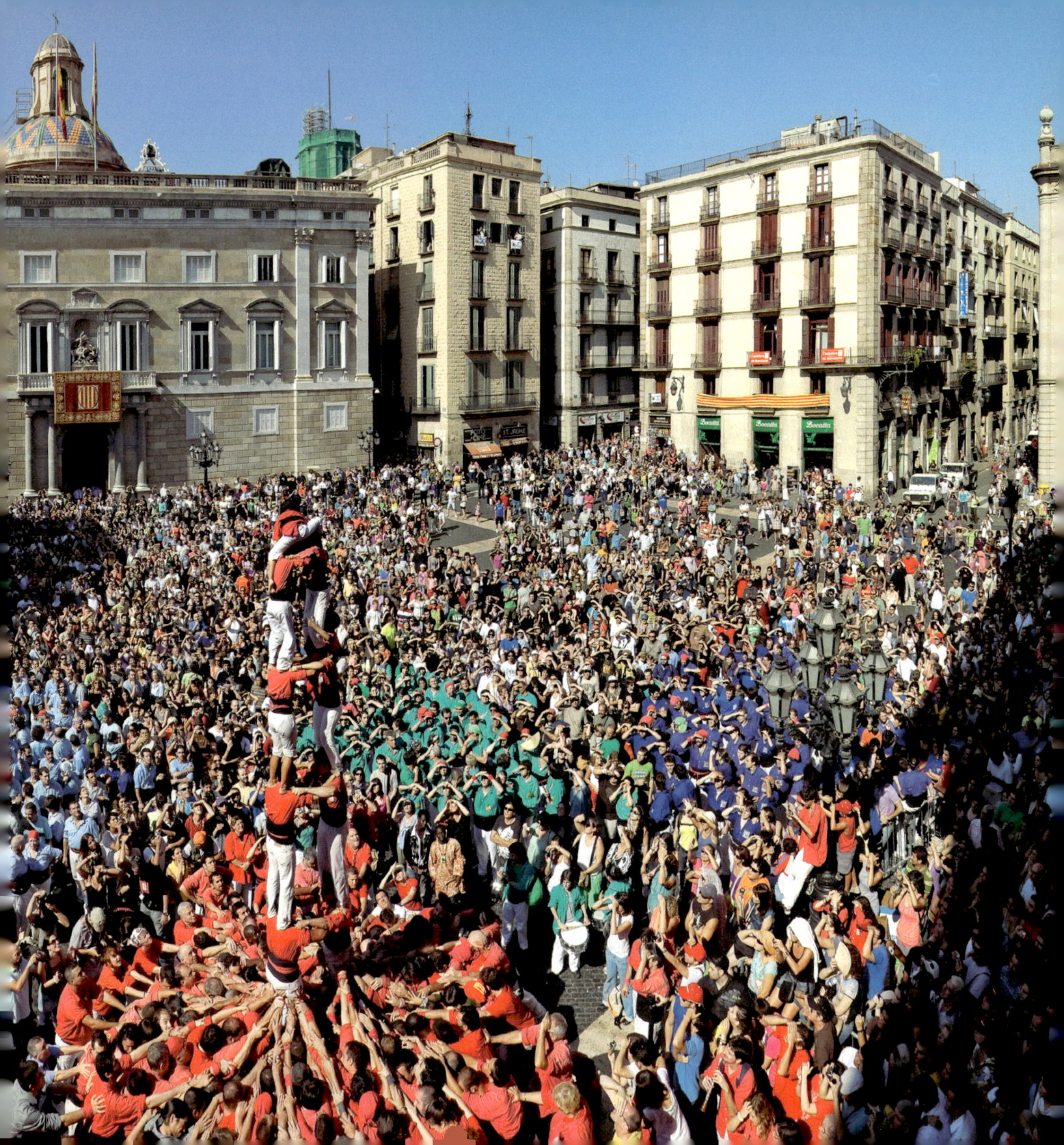

Nens del Vendrell. El Vendrell

Marrecs de Salt. Plaça del Vi. Girona

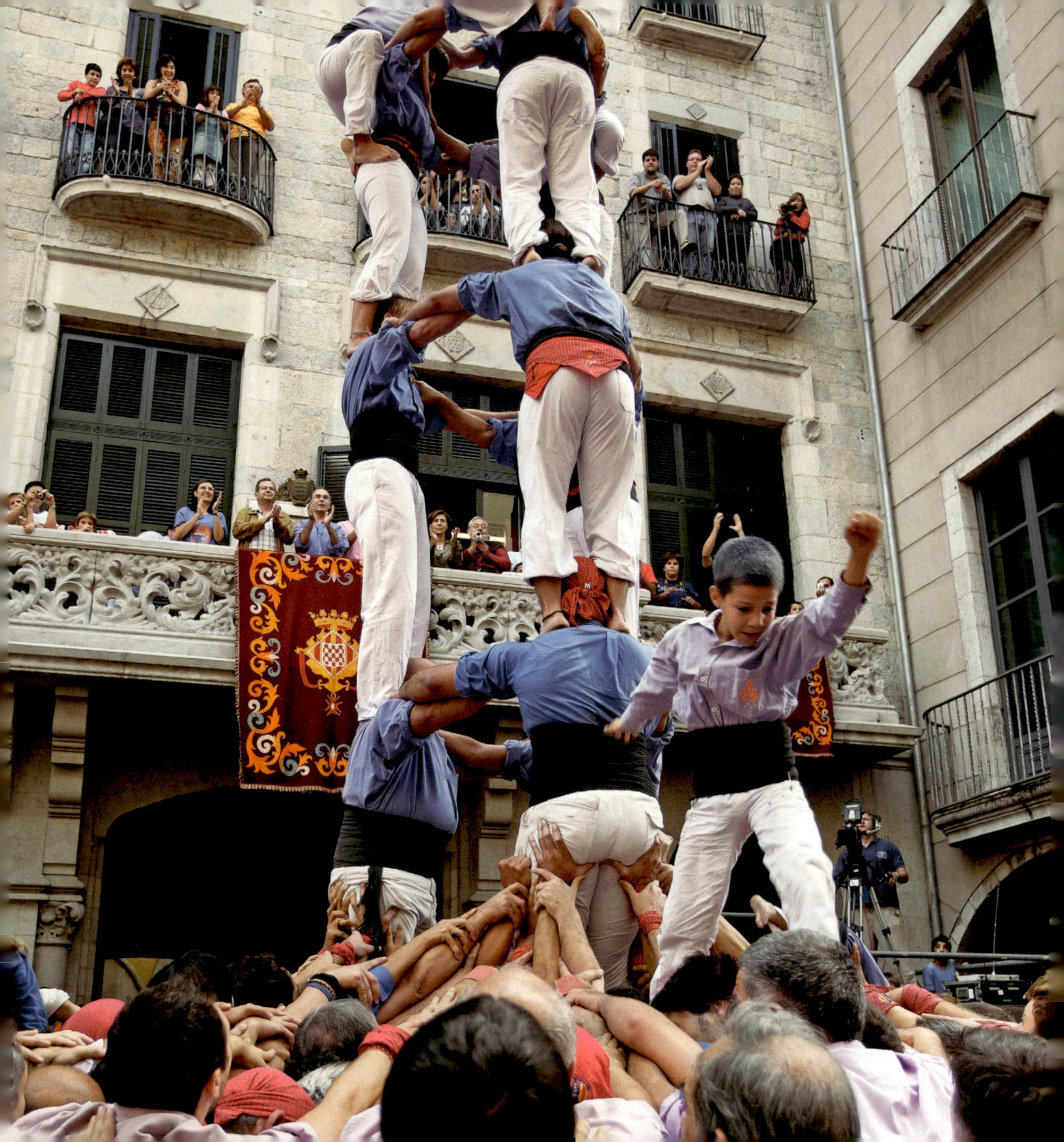

# **1.** Getting our bearings

Pillars

4 of 7 _ Colles de l'Eix

**Decennial Festivals of the Virgin of the Candela. Valls, 30 January 2011.**
As the name indicates, the Decennial Festivals are held every ten years in Valls, the town considered the birthplace of the first *colles castelleres*. For these festivals, it is traditional to invite all the other *colles* to raise a *pilar* in the Plaça del Blat, setting of the great exploits of the local *colles* and where, with the exception of this day, only they can perform. In another place in the town, all the *colles* taking part in the decennials use the day to raise their first *castells* of the year.

Al·lots de Llevant

**1.** Getting our bearings

# Competition of *Castells* of Tarragona

No *casteller* or fan wants to miss this *diada*. It is held every two years, always on an even year, on the first Sunday of October. It is the big event of the *casteller* world, the veritable "Casteller World Cup", as some journalists have called it. For many, it is like a big sporting final. The best *colles* of the moment take part, which classify according to the merit of their performances and of the *castells* they have raised during the first half of the season. It is held in the city of Tarragona, in the auditorium called Tarraco Arena Plaza (the old bullfighting ring), a special setting and, at the same time, different from the other events, where the public are spectators in the stands and the *colles*, and fans wishing to cooperate, are in the central circular space. It is the only event where the public must pay a modest sum and it lasts for more than four hours. The *colles* will try and win the competition or achieve the best position taking into account their level. The cash prizes they win are substantial, but the prestige they gain is even greater. The competition has its own rules and a points table for the *castells* achieved that you can consult on its web page (www.concursdecastells.cat). Broadly speaking, and unlike the conventional *diades castelleres*, in the competition only the best three *castells* made by each *colla* will be counted for points, and the *colles* are penalised when they are not formed in the orthodox way. You can also buy tickets for the event in advance from this website, or consult the classification table of the *colles* that leads to entry to the competition, or get it direct online. The majority of the media in Catalonia give special coverage and television and radio broadcast it live with special articles by the written press. It is an almost unique spectacle of colour. Don't miss it!

Xiquets de Reus, Xics de Granollers and Sagals d'Osona. Competition of *Castells* of Tarragona. 2004

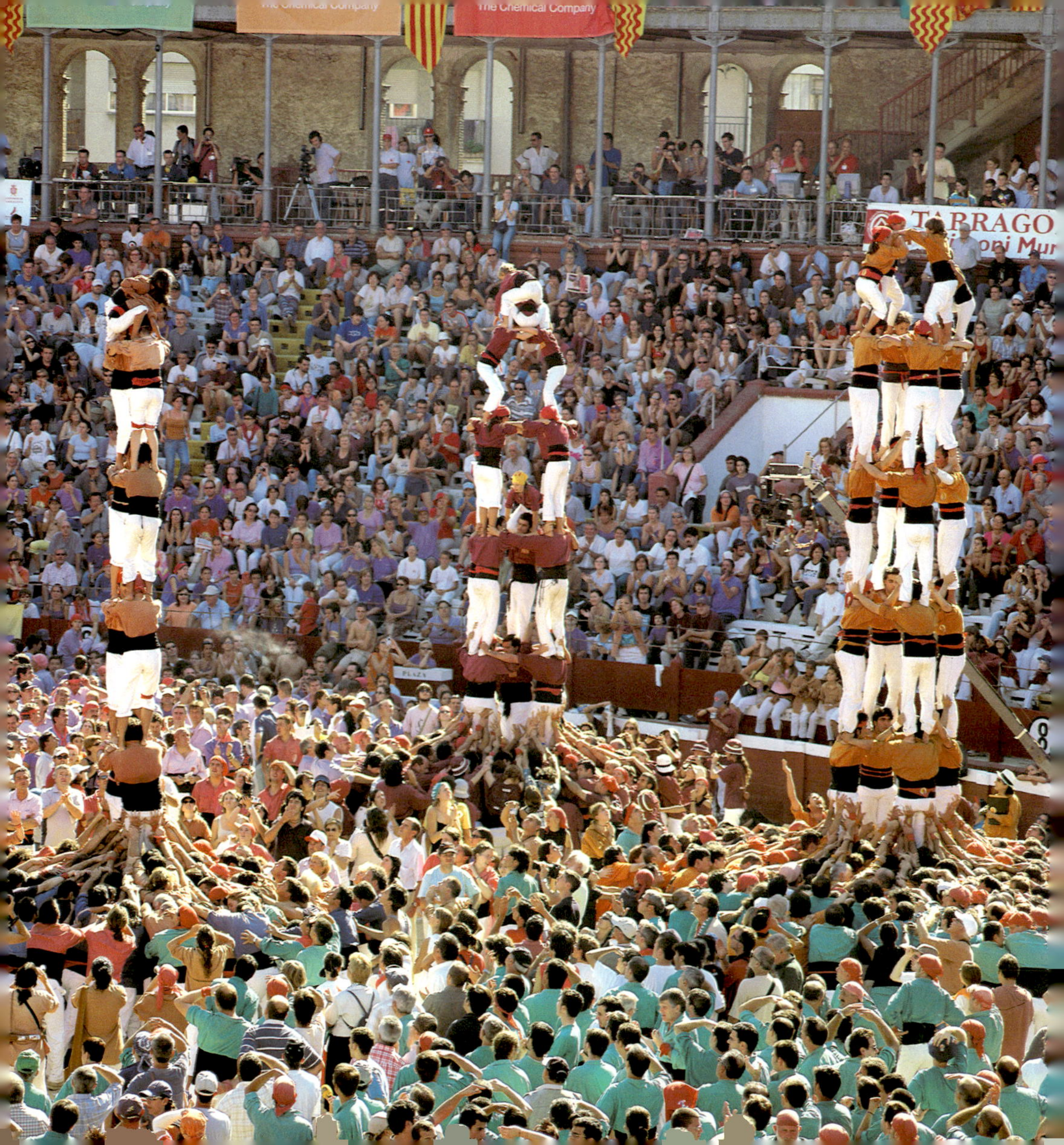
The Chemical Company
The Chemical Company
TARRAGO

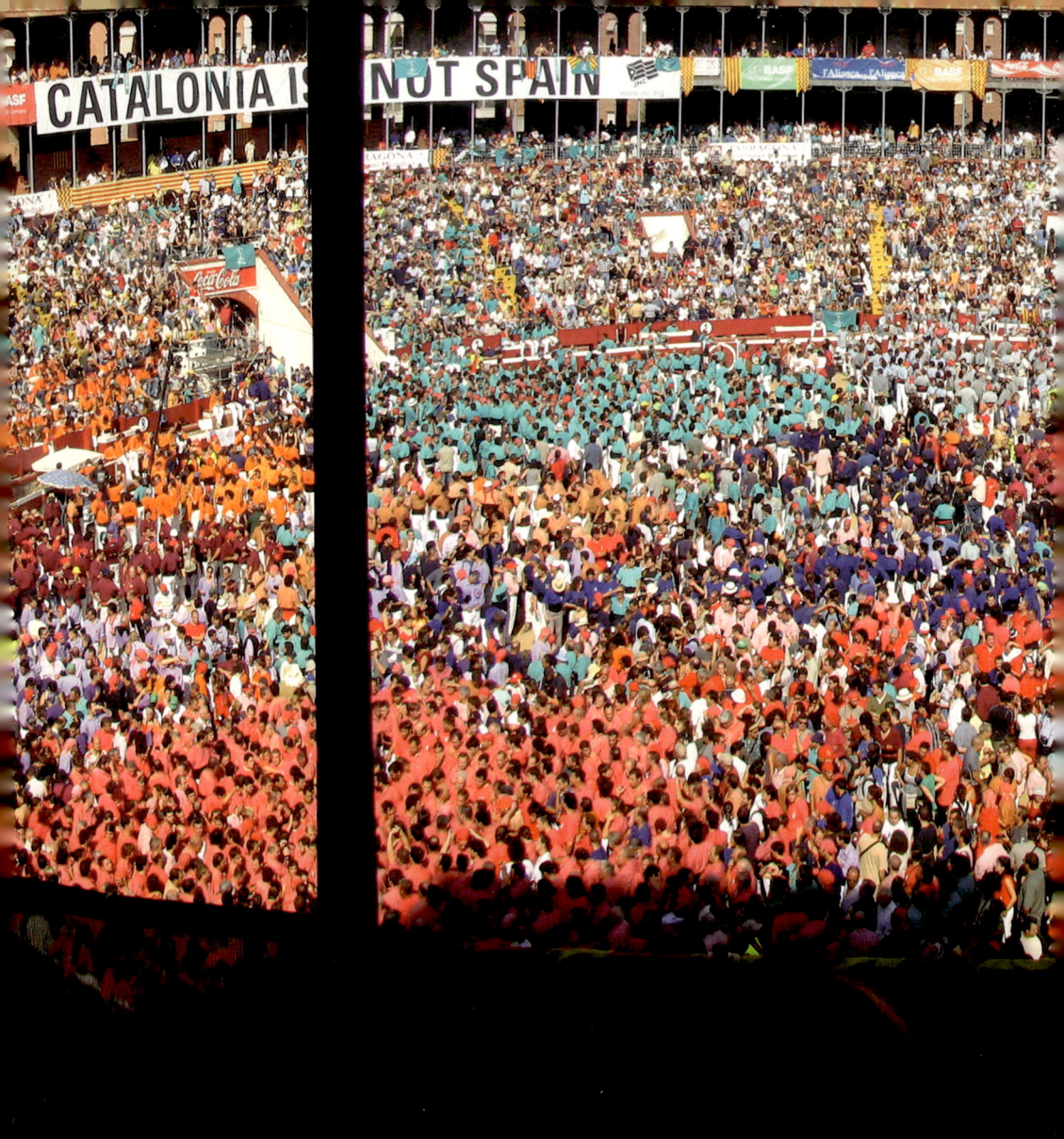

CATALONIA IS NOT SPAIN

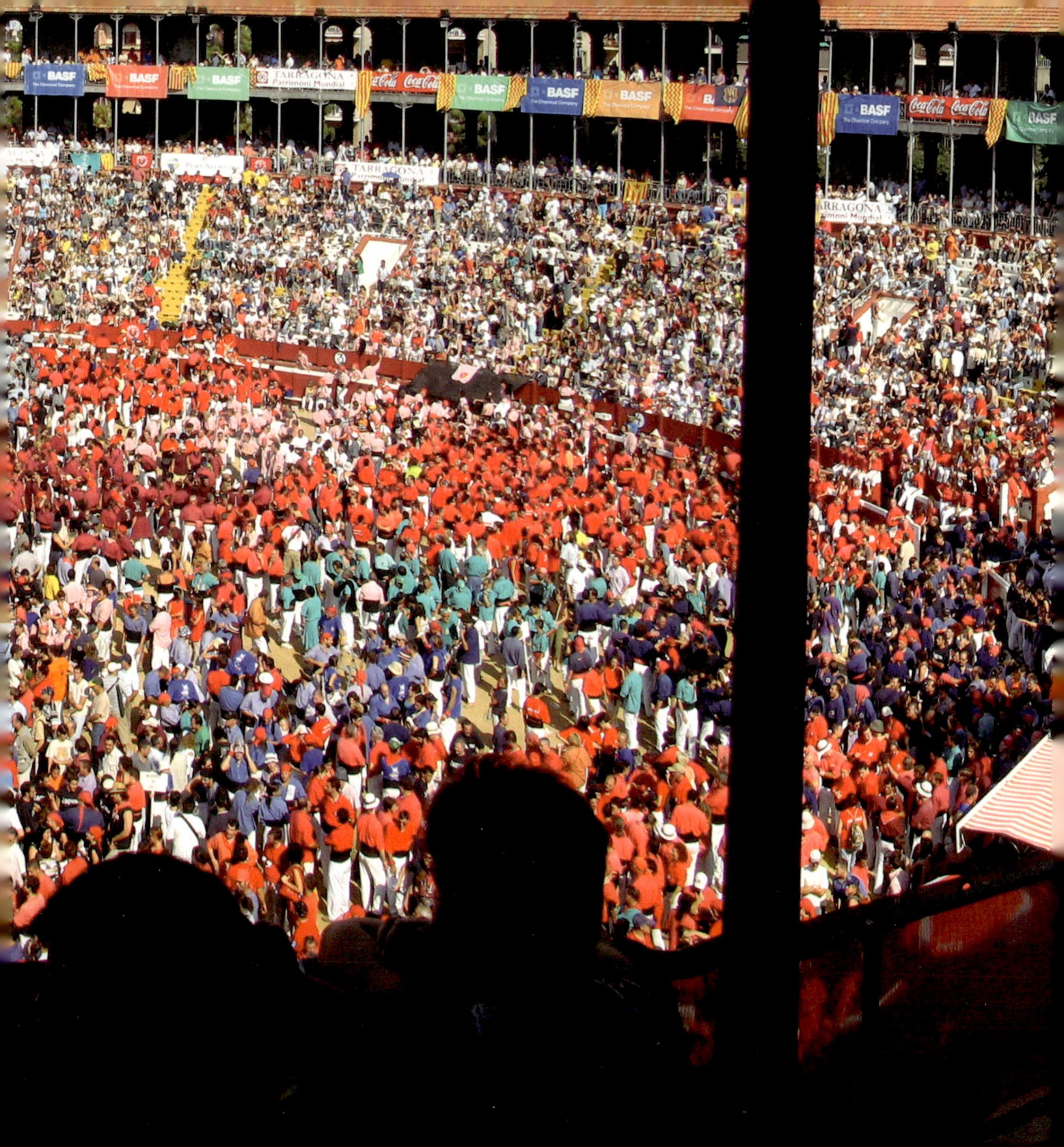
BASF
TARRAGONA
Patrimoni Mundial
Coca-Cola

Colla Vella dels Xiquets de Valls

Colla Joves Xiquets de Valls

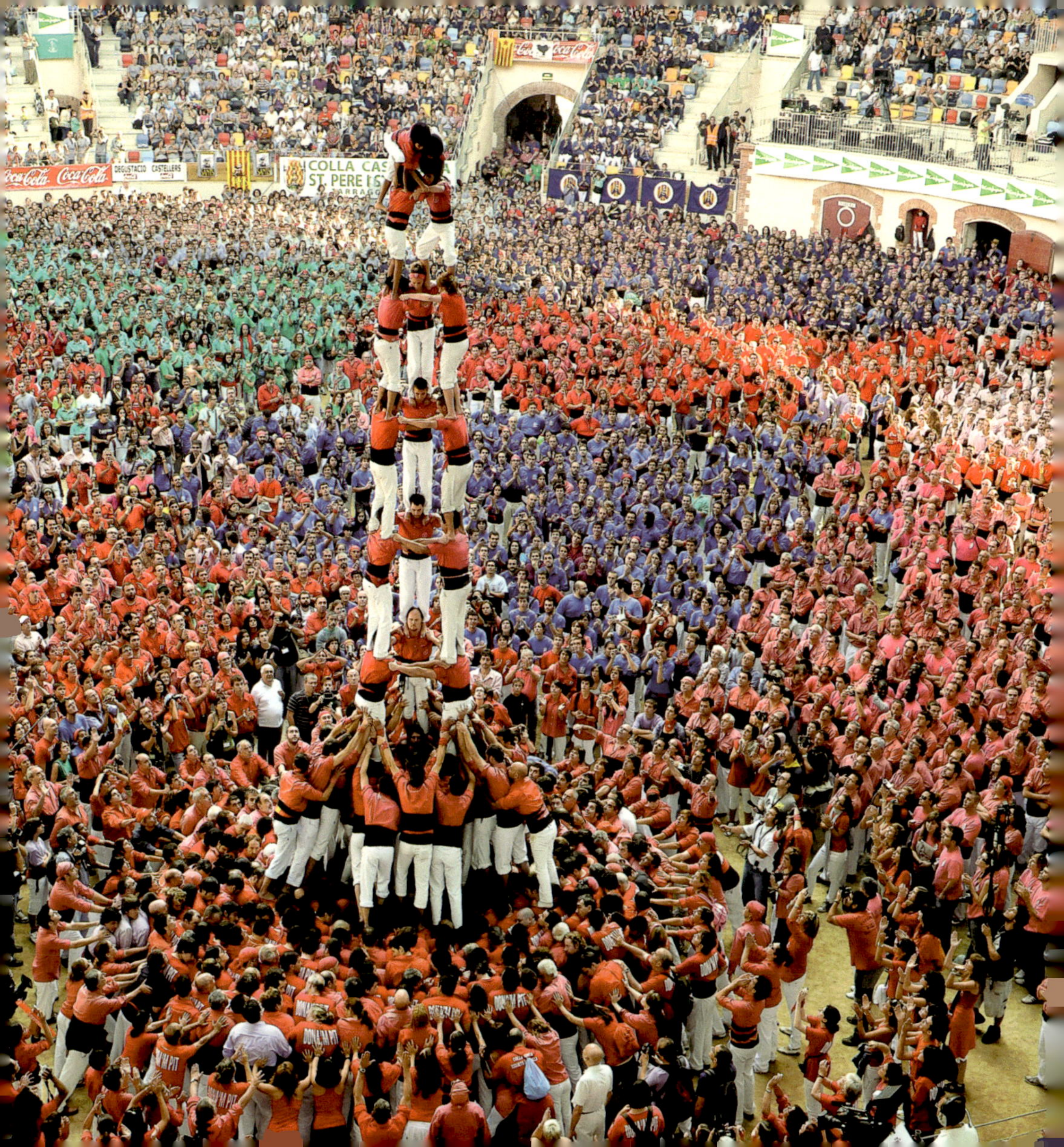
Coca-Cola
Coca-Cola
COLLA CAS
ST. PERE I S

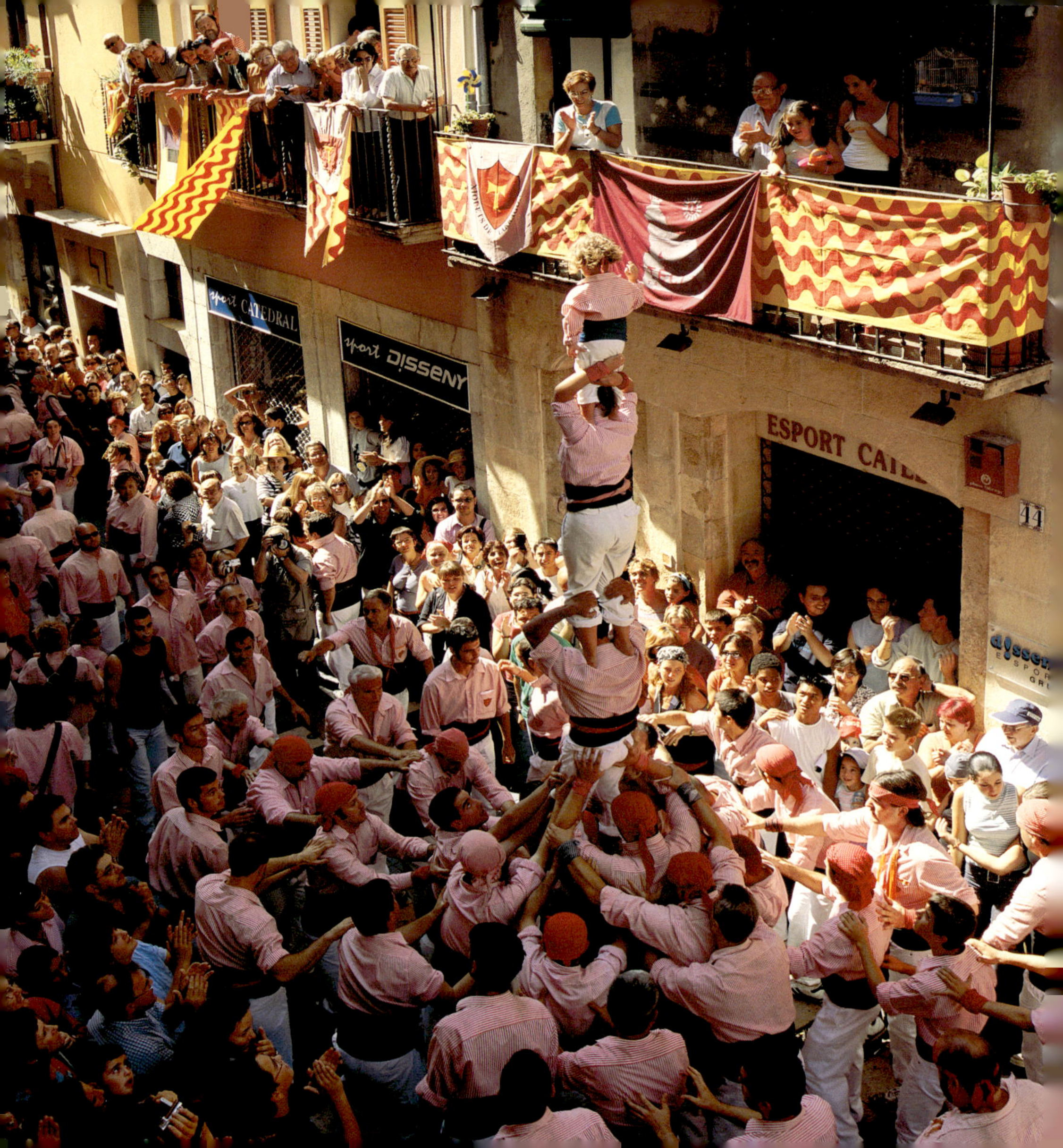
sport CATEDRAL
sport DISSENY
ESPORT
44

# The route of the *castells*

Cities and towns with outstanding *casteller* performances

- Perpinyà
- Figueres
- Olot
- Girona
- Vic
- Granollers
- Mataró
- Vilassar de Dalt
- Igualada
- Terrassa
- Premià de Mar
- Lleida
- Sabadell
- Cornellà
- Badalona
- Barcelona
- Vilafranca del Penedès
- Montblanc
- Llorenç del Penedès
- Vila-rodona
- La Bisbal del Penedès
- Valls
- L'Arboç
- La Selva del Camp
- El Vendrell
- Sitges
- Calafell
- Vilanova i la Geltrú
- Reus
- El Catllar
- Torredembarra
- Altafulla
- Tarragona
- Manacor
- Palma de Mallorca

Pillar of 4 walking _ Xiquets de Tarragona. Carrer Major. Tarragona

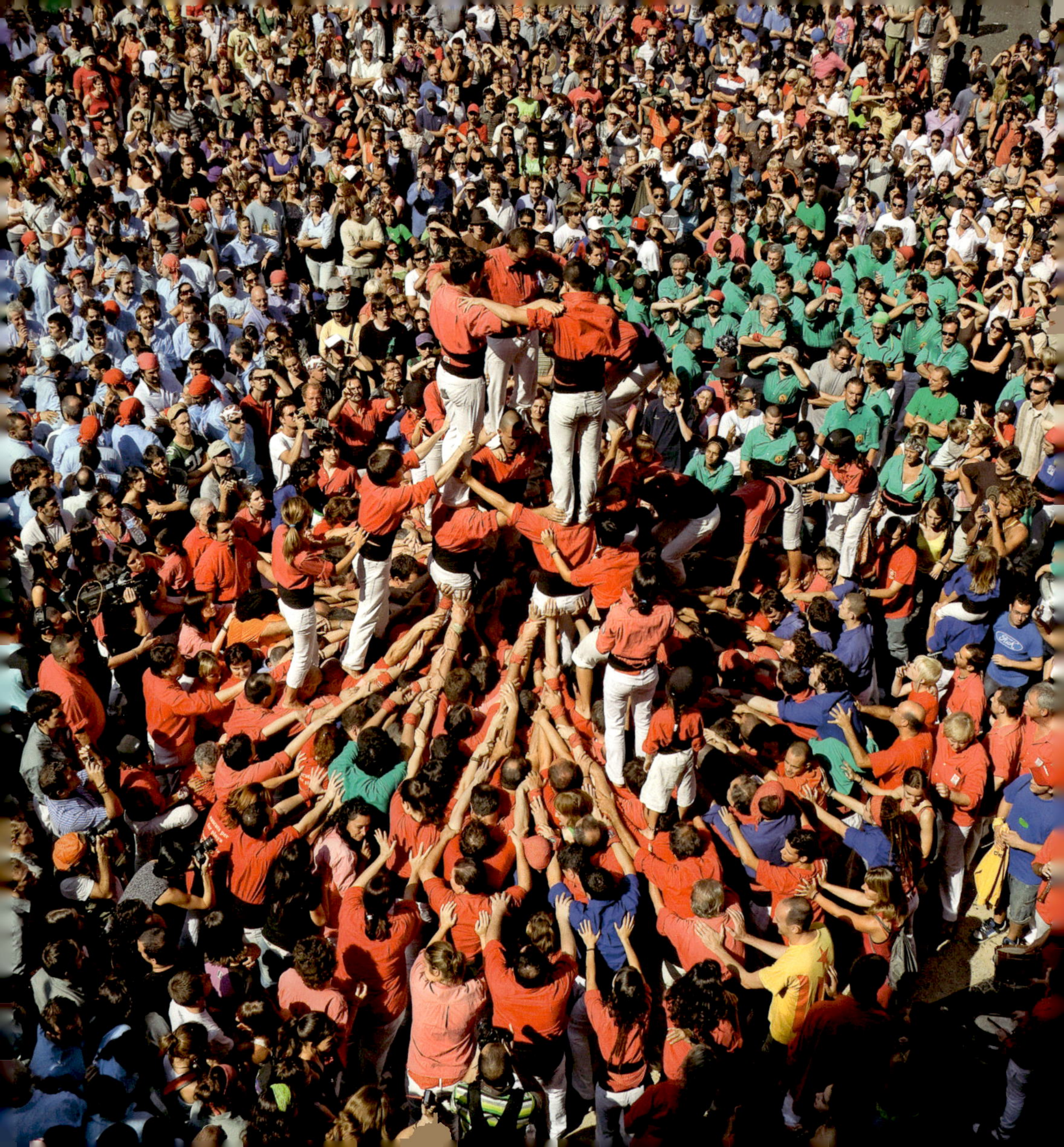

# 2. Let's enjoy it
## How and from where we can see the *castells*

On a *diada castellera* you can see people watching from windows and balconies. It is comfortable, but not to everyone's taste. Some people say that the *castells* must be seen from the ground, and that from this perspective you get a better idea of the nuances and sensations they transmit. In any case, and more so if you don't know anyone to invite you up to a balcony, the simplest thing to do is arrive at the setting of the *casteller* and, at the same level, try and find the best spot. Do you want to take part in the *pinyes*? Well, just stand close to the *colles* and tell them you want to collaborate. Do you want to take photos or film? Then choose the best spot according to the capabilities of your equipment. We should point out, however, that the *castells* have a profile and perfect moments for being photographed. Generally, the crowning moment is captured forever, the moment when the person who climbs to the top raises their hand, when in a *castell* with a complex structure this gesture is repeated more than once, the last one should be photographed. One more thing: you should photograph the *castell* from the angle that enables you to see the face of the young *casteller* who salutes, who does the *aleta*. Do you want to see and experience close-up the effort and struggle of the *castellers*? You should place yourself a few metres from the *pinya* and you will be able to hear the instructions that the heads of the *castell* give, some of the words that the *castellers* exchange, the concentrated stares, the expressions of effort, and the exclamations of joy when they achieve an important feat. Do you want to see the spectacle in the utmost comfort? Then look for the least crowded spot and, if it is the middle of summer, where there is some shade. Perhaps in this way you will not find the heart of the *diada*, but you will be able to get a more overall view of the event.

**2.** Let's enjoy it

Colla Joves Xiquets de Valls

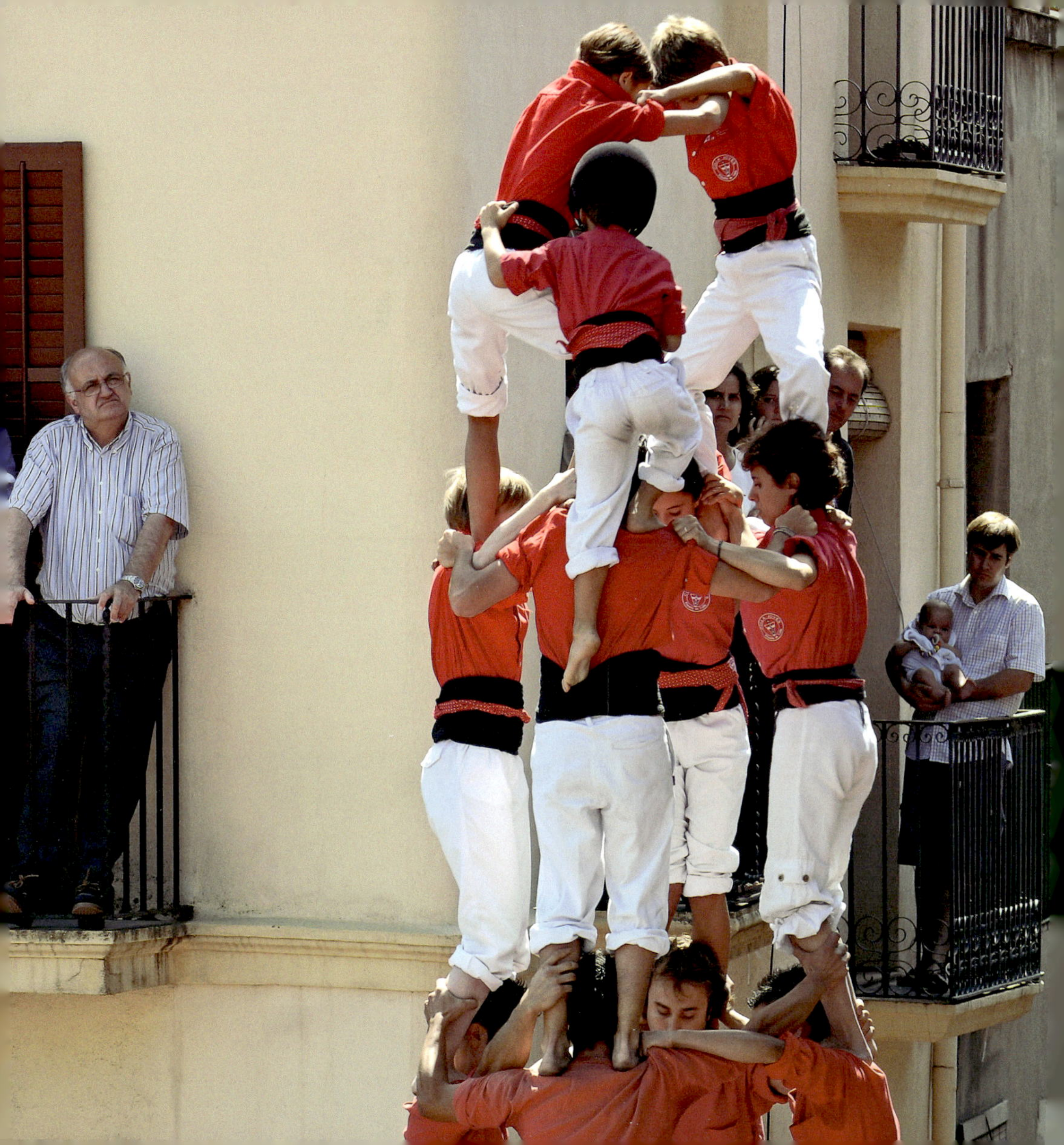

**2.** Let's enjoy it

Castellers de Vilafranca

Minyons de Terrassa

50

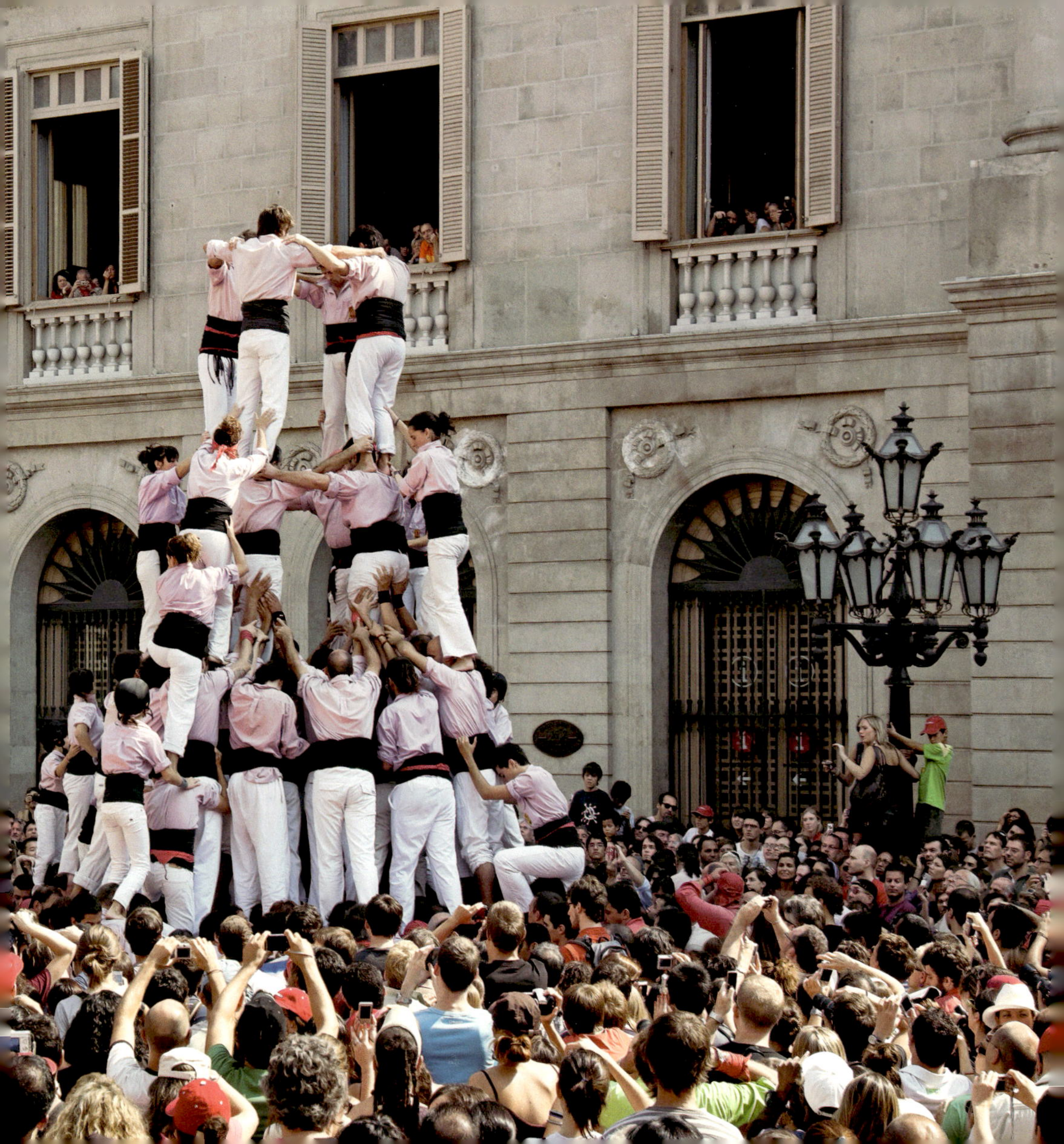

## 2. Let's enjoy it

# *Castells* in summer

The majority of the *diades* are concentrated in summer, the months of June, July, August and September, when the weather is the warmest in Catalonia. This is a consequence, to a large extent, of tradition. In Catalonia the majority of local festivals have historically been concentrated in the months with good weather, and the *castells* arose as essential elements of these festivals. It is also the case, however, that the cold does not encourage the presence of spectators in the open air, or the physical performance of the *castellers*, who must have their muscles fully toned up, especially the legs, arms and hands. Therefore, taking into account that a *diada* may last two or more hours, we should get there a little in advance to get a good view, and if we want, a shady area. Seeing as this is often not possible, it is a good idea to take a cap or hat —never a sunshade because we will obscure the view of the people behind us. It is also a very good idea to take water so we do not dehydrate. However, as the *castells* are also made in November, a month in which it is already cold, if we want to help a *colla* by forming part of the *pinyes*, the warm clothing we wear should be the lightest possible.

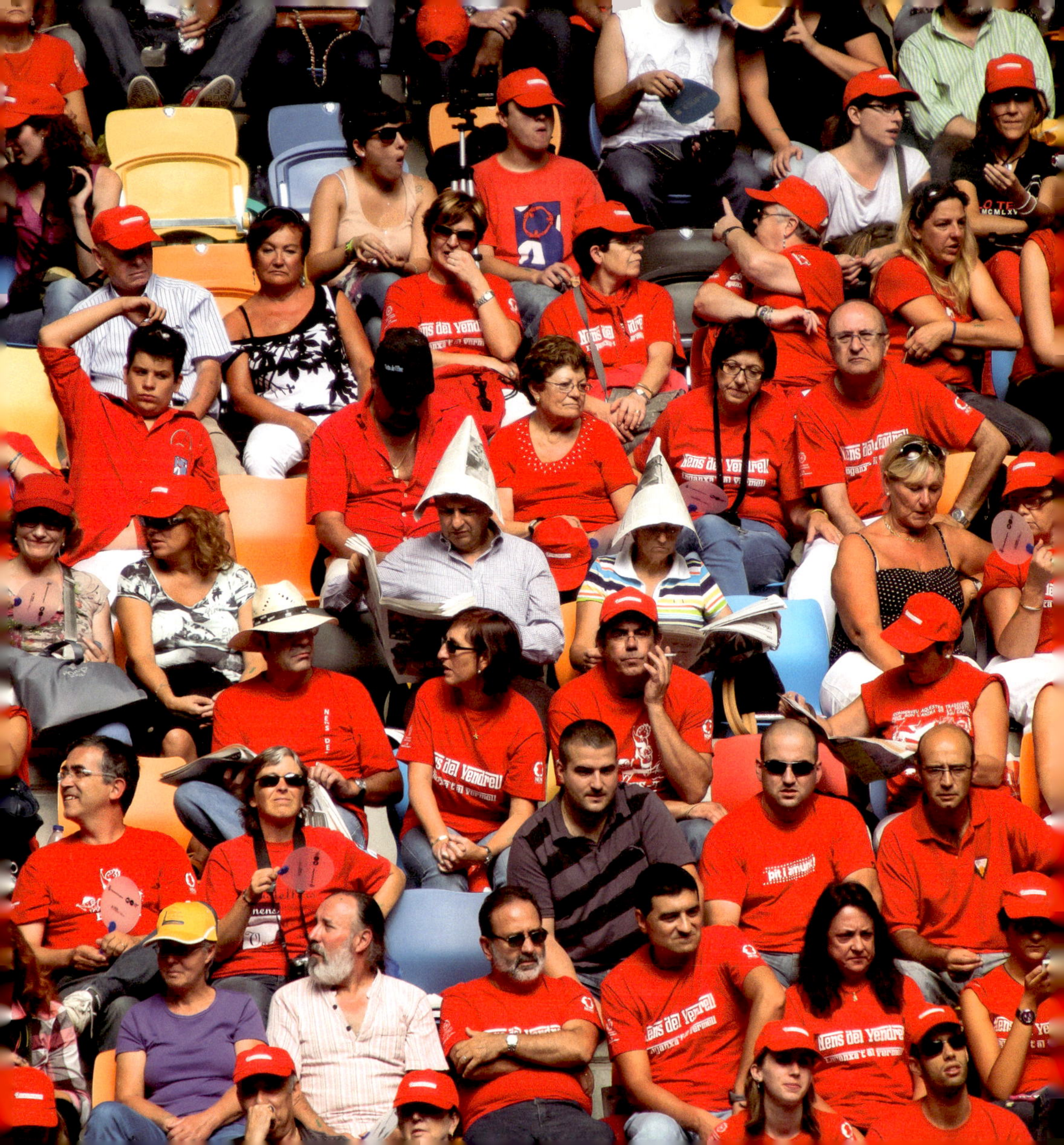
Nens del Vendrell
pit i amunt!

**2.** Let's enjoy it

# Taking part in a *castell*

The public who attend a *diada* can always help the *colles* to make the *castell*, and in fact this has always been the case. Today, the place reserved for the fans is always at the base, that is the *pinya*, unlike in the 19th century in particular, when the original *colles* had volunteers in the towns where they performed who climbed up the *castell*. Before becoming involved and positioning ourselves, it is always a good idea to ask a *casteller* from the *colla* we want to support in what position we can help them the most, or how we should place our arms. It is very important that, as a measure of caution, we support our head well on the shoulder of the *casteller* we have before us and that we do not look up. This way we will avoid injuring ourselves if there is a collapse of the upper storeys onto the area of the *pinya* where we are situated. In the inside of a *pinya* we can experience different sensations, even feeling more like participants.

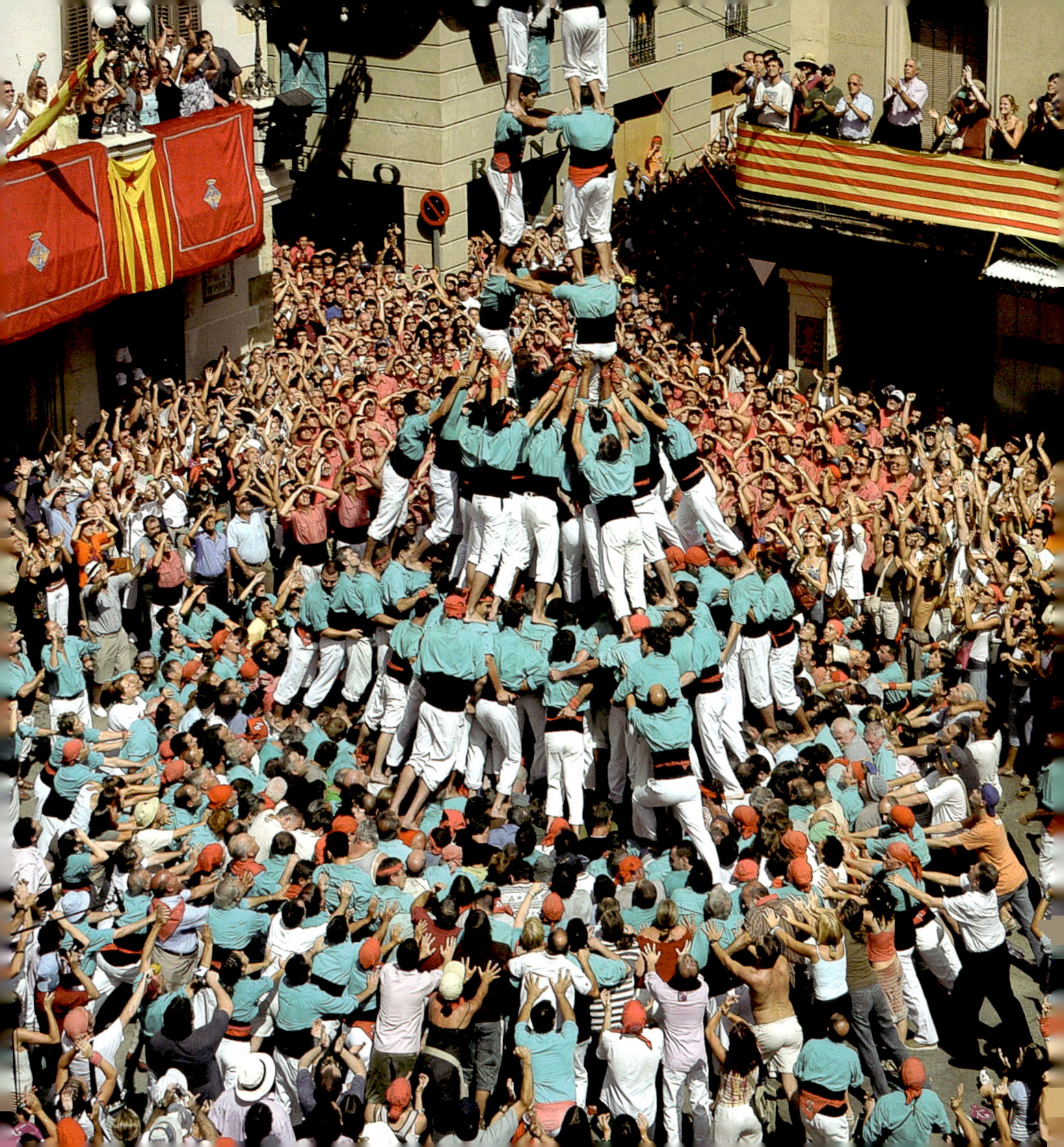

**2.** Let's enjoy it

# Experiencing the atmosphere of the *castellers*

It is advisable to arrive at the setting of the *diada* half an hour before it is due to start. This is not only to find the spot we want more easily, but also to be able to ask the *castellers* or other fans which *castells* we will be able to see. Thus we will be able to follow the day's events more closely, and to be fully aware of what is going on. For example, we could find out how the rehearsals have been of each *colla* before attempting a big challenge. When the *diades* are at midday, many *castellers* and fans meet before the event in nearby bars and cafes for a drink or breakfast. We can go and take part in this *casteller* atmosphere since they are usually open people, who like to explain aspects related to their and others' *colles*.

Minyons de Terrassa

Colla Vella dels Xiquets de Valls heading for the Plaça del Blat in Valls in formation

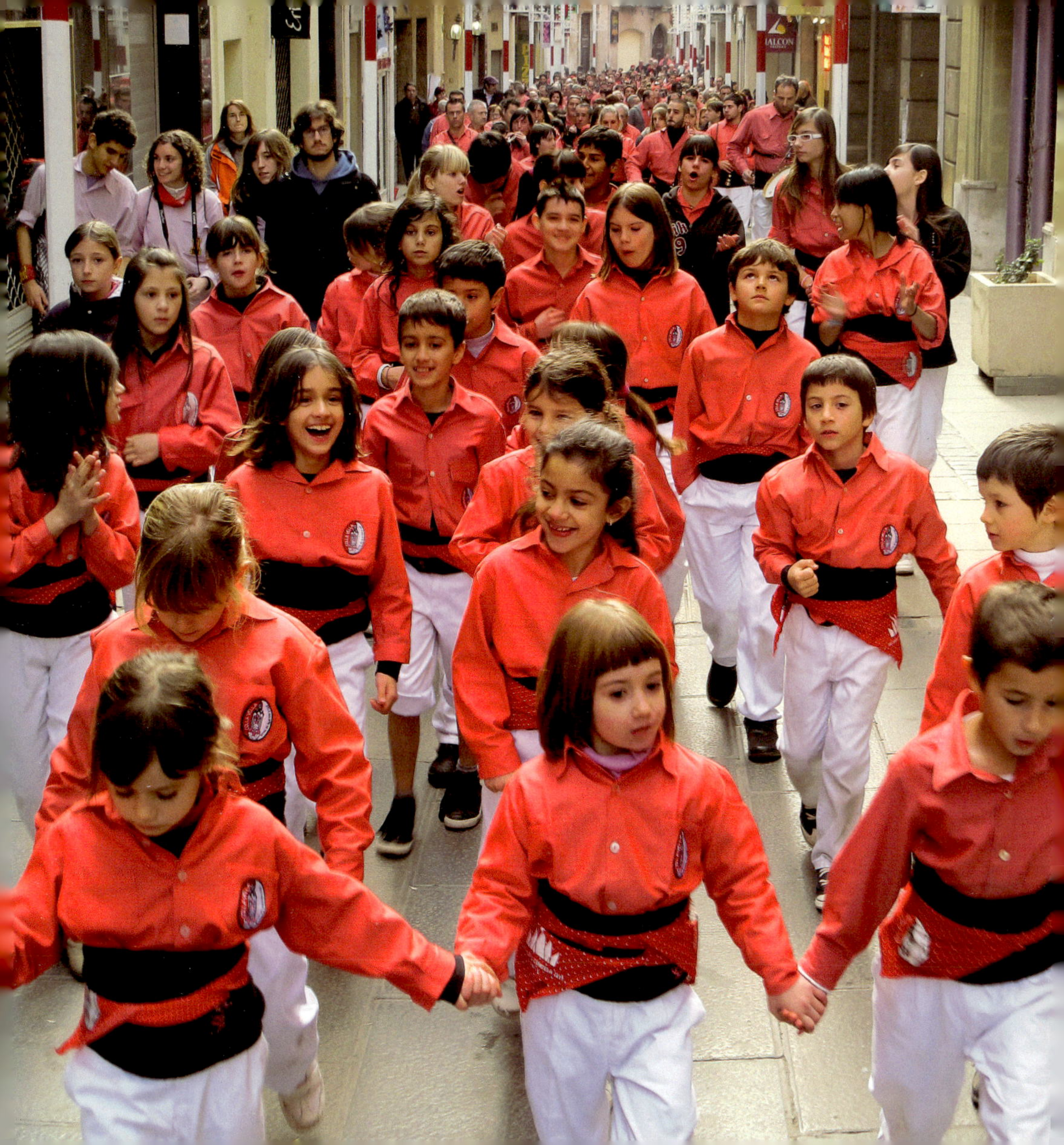
HALCON

Pillar of 4 walking _ Castellers de Lleida

Pillar of 4 walking _ Castellers del Poble Sec

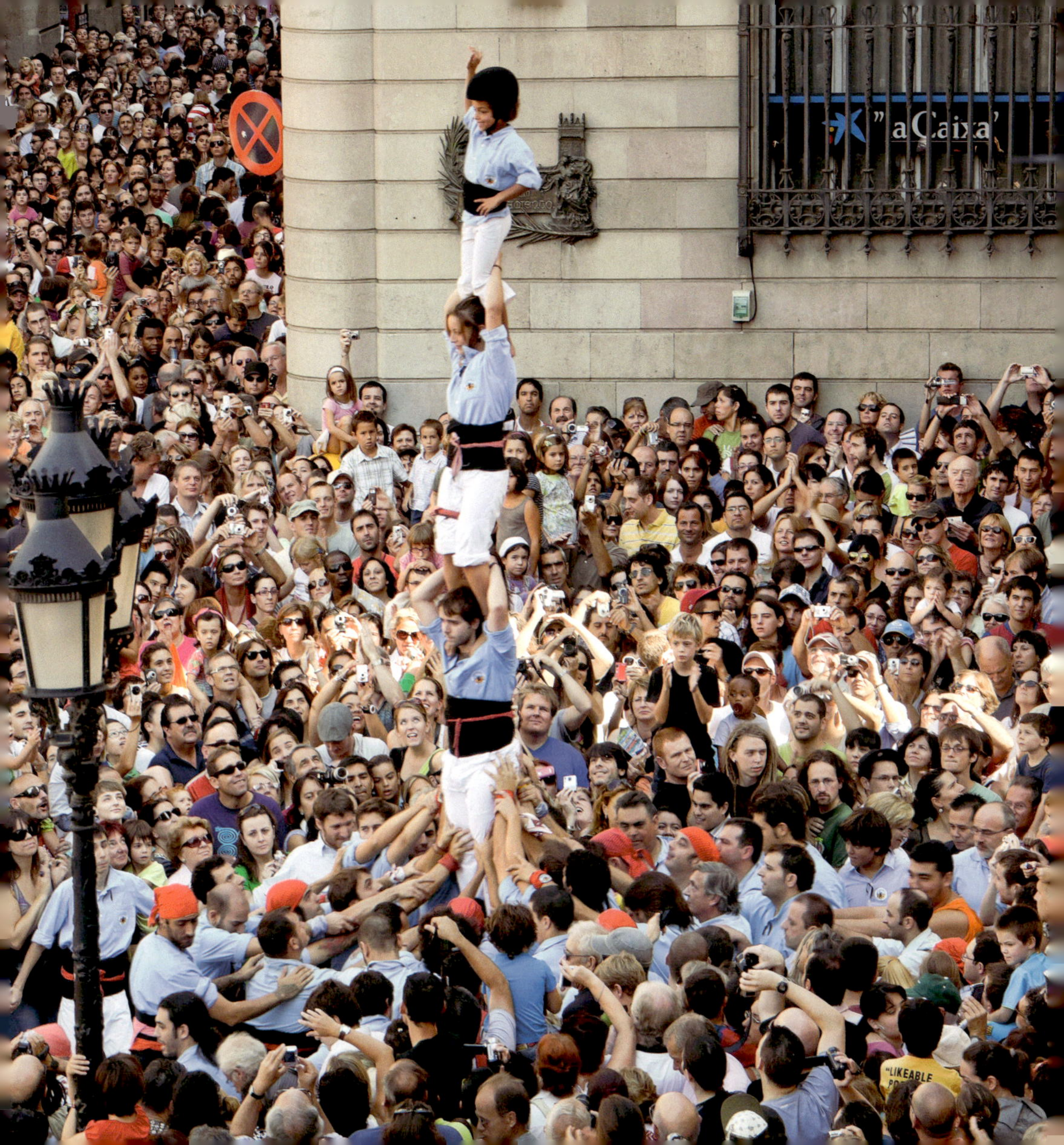
"aCaixa"

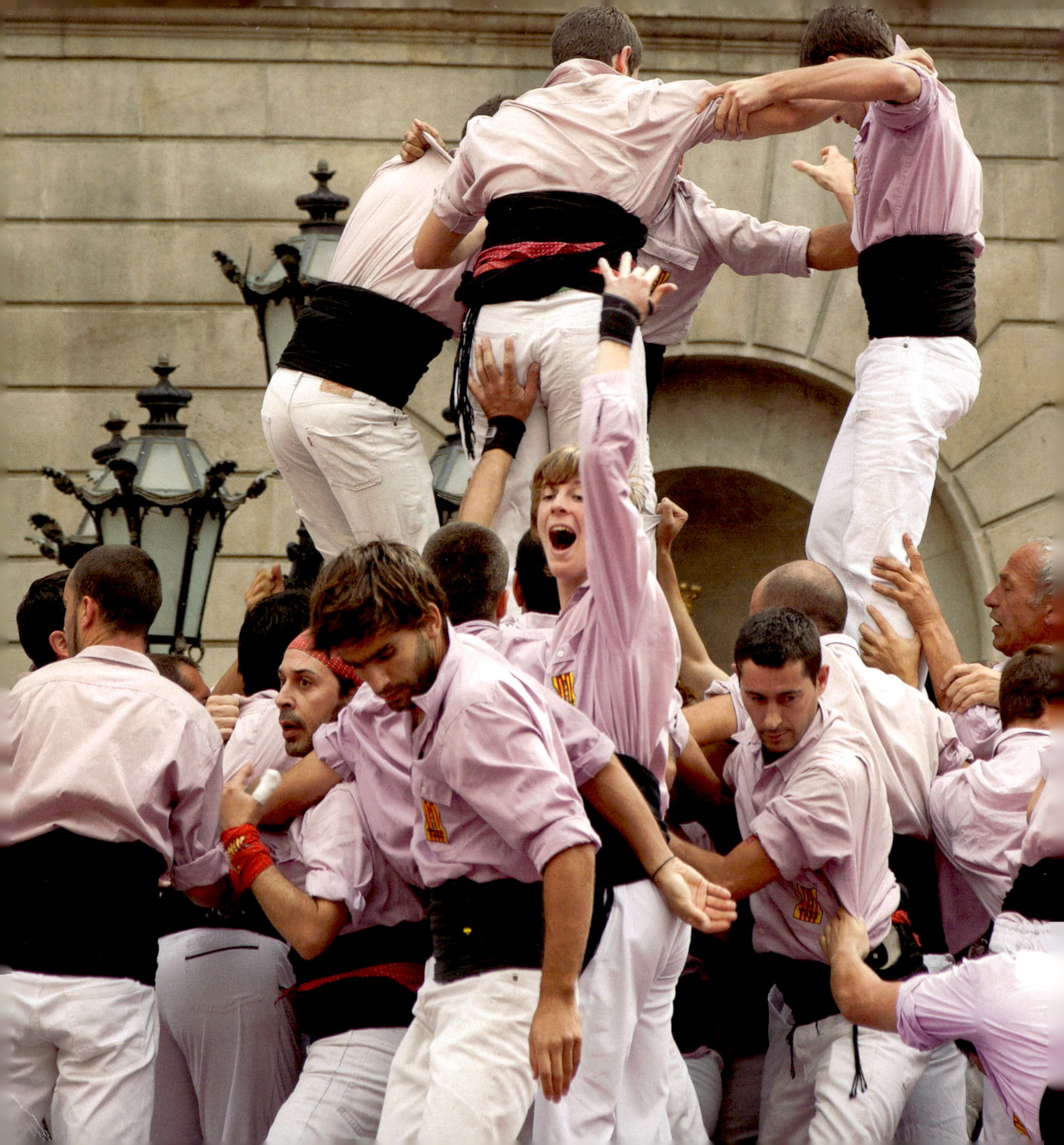

# 3. The *castellers*

This is the name given to the members of a *colla* and who wear its shirt. However, the *castellers* may have very different functions within the same *colla*, from administrative functions to purely *casteller* activity. There are therefore people in charge of the logistics of the travel, responsible for the accounts, material, or those who focus on the physical activity of the *castells*. Basically, the direction of a *colla* is made up of a technical and administrative team, both chosen by vote among the *castellers* of the *colla*. There may be several specialisations within the technical team, such as a team focused on the training of *la canalla* (the boys and girls), a team that works on the *pilar*, or there may be another that is in charge of rehearsing with the *castellers* of the *tronc*, and another specialised in forming the *pinya*, the *folre* and the *manilles*. These teams are often led by experienced *castellers*, who had formed part of one of these positions or elements of the *castells*, or who continue forming part.

**3.** The *castellers*

Castellers de Vilafranca

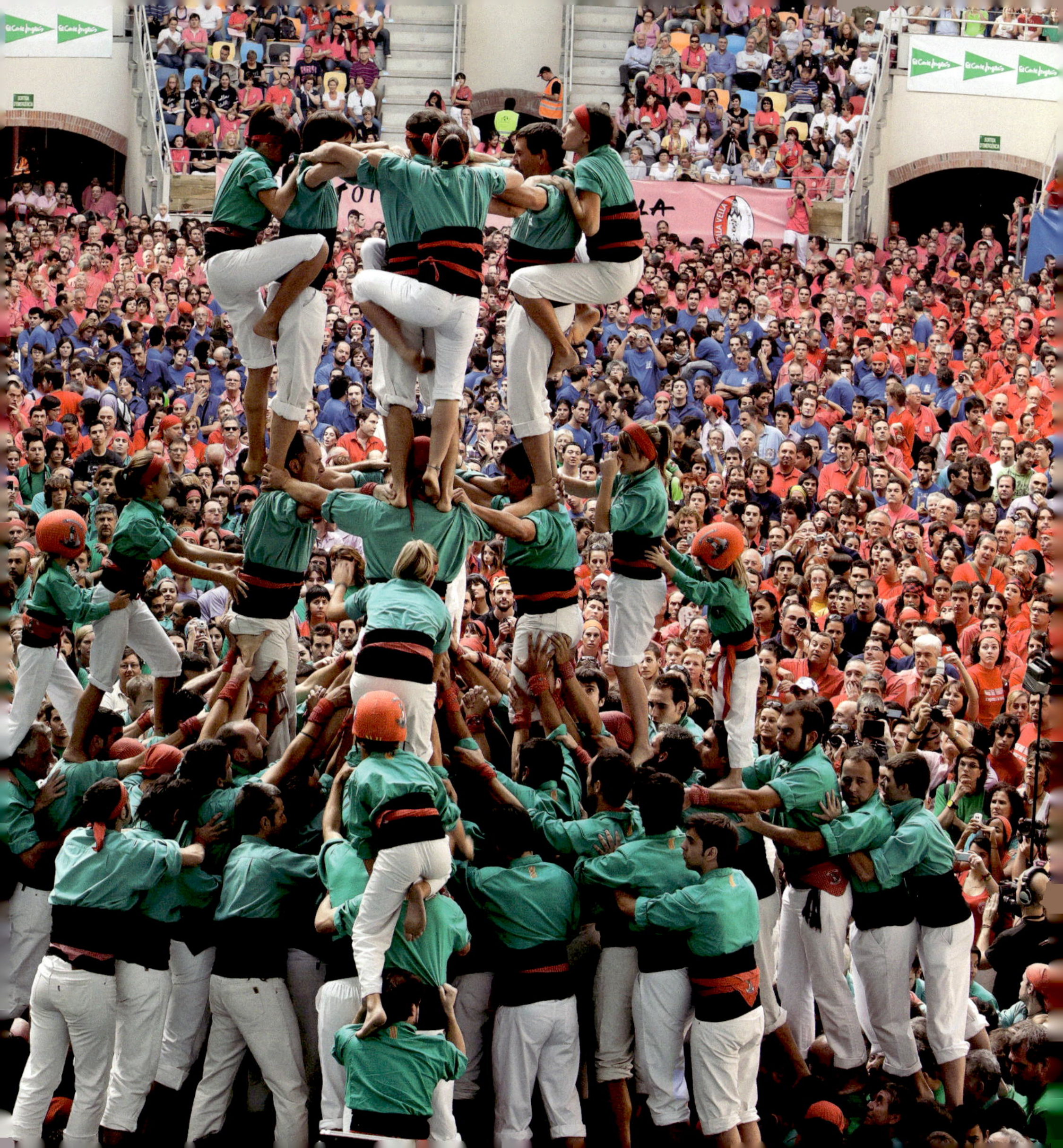

**3.** The *castellers*

# An intergenerational world

For the *castells* there is almost no age limit. There are *enxanetes* and *aixecadors* of only six or seven, and *castellers* who take part in the *pinyes* who are over seventy. It is also true that for many of the positions of a *castell* you must have great physical strength combined with a good command of the technique. In this sense, therefore, physical fitness, body size, weight, command of the technique, but also the mentality, determine the position of each *casteller*.

**3.** The *castellers*

**3.** The *castellers*

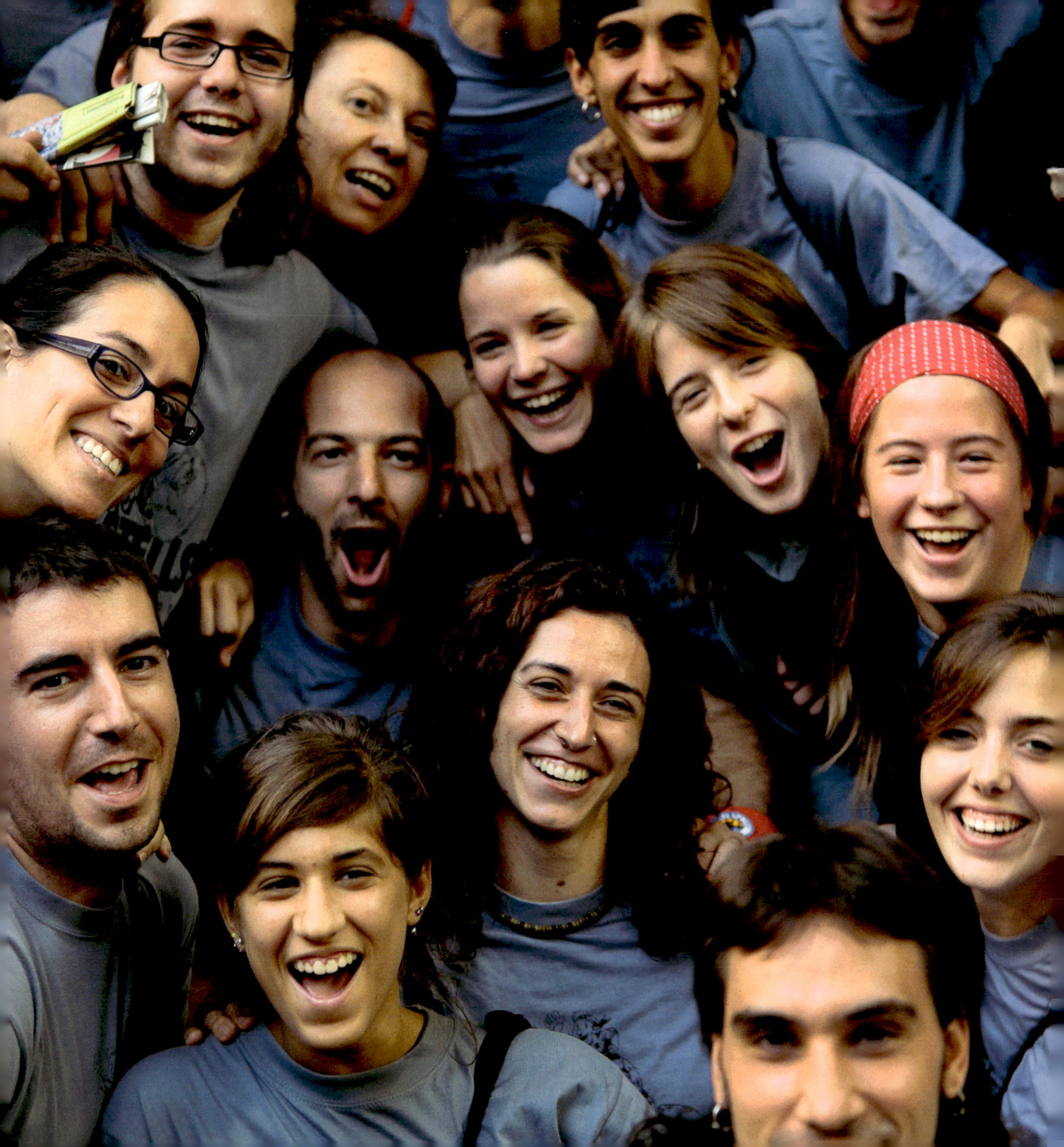

**3.** The *castellers*

Castellers de Sants

*Enxanetes* of the Bordegassos de Vilanova waiting before climbing up the *castell*

# The youngsters

*Els castells els fan la canalla* (The youngsters make the *castells*). This is undoubtedly the most popular saying, and well founded, in the *casteller* world. It means that without the youngest ones, without those that climb up to the top, a *castell* cannot be made and that whether a *castell* becomes an attempt or not depends on whether they, especially the *enxaneta*, want to climb or not. For this reason, the *castellers* of the *pom de dalt*, made up of the *dosos*, the *aixecador* and the *enxaneta*, are those that receive most consideration in a *colla*, as they are often the true heroes, also for the public. The main qualities of an *enxaneta* and an *aixecador* are agility, skill and bravery climbing up and down a *castell*.

Castellers de Barcelona

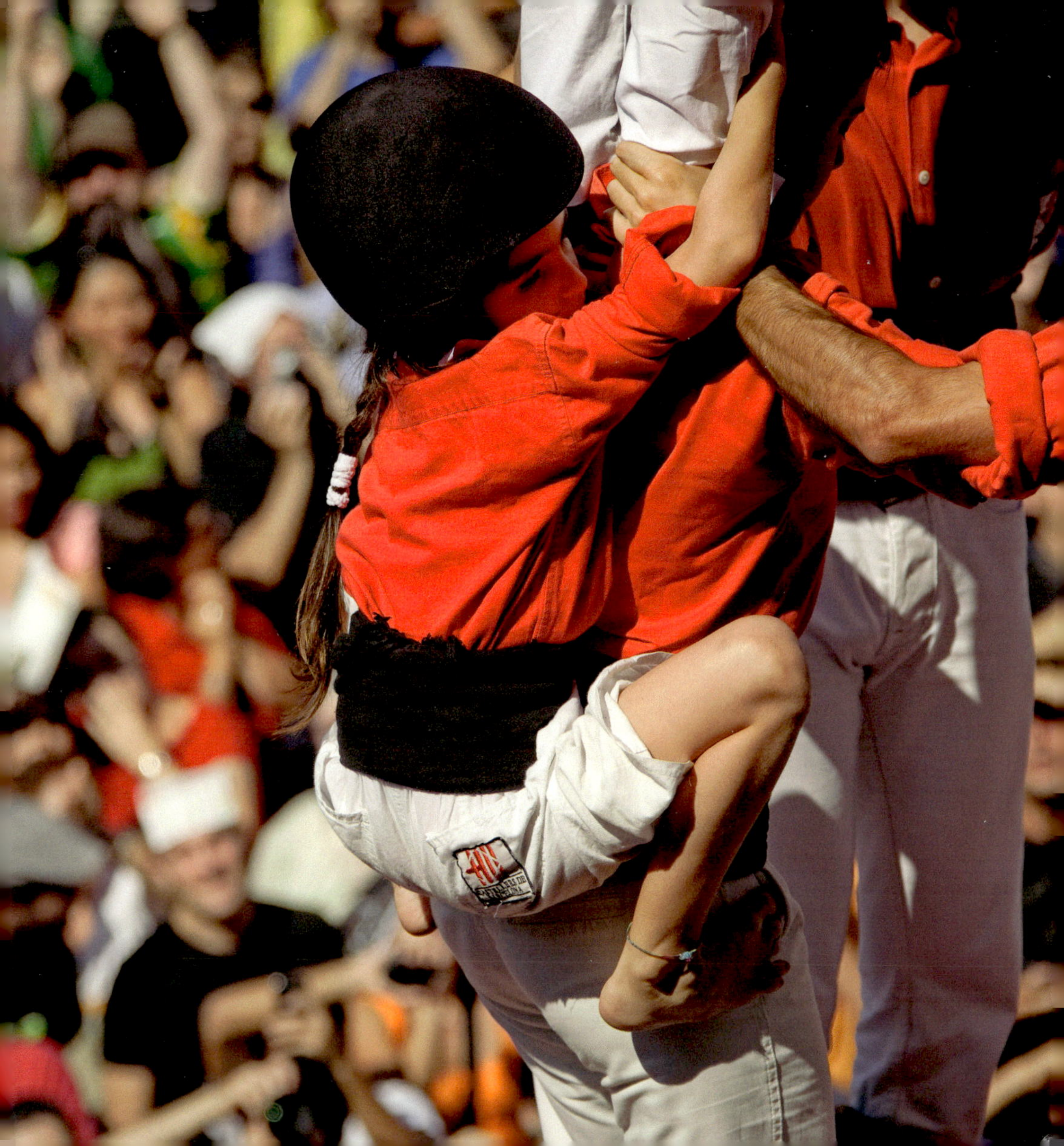

Castellers de Sant Cugat

**3.** The *castellers*

Nens del Vendrell

**3.** The *castellers*

Castellers de Vilafranca

Minyons de Terrassa

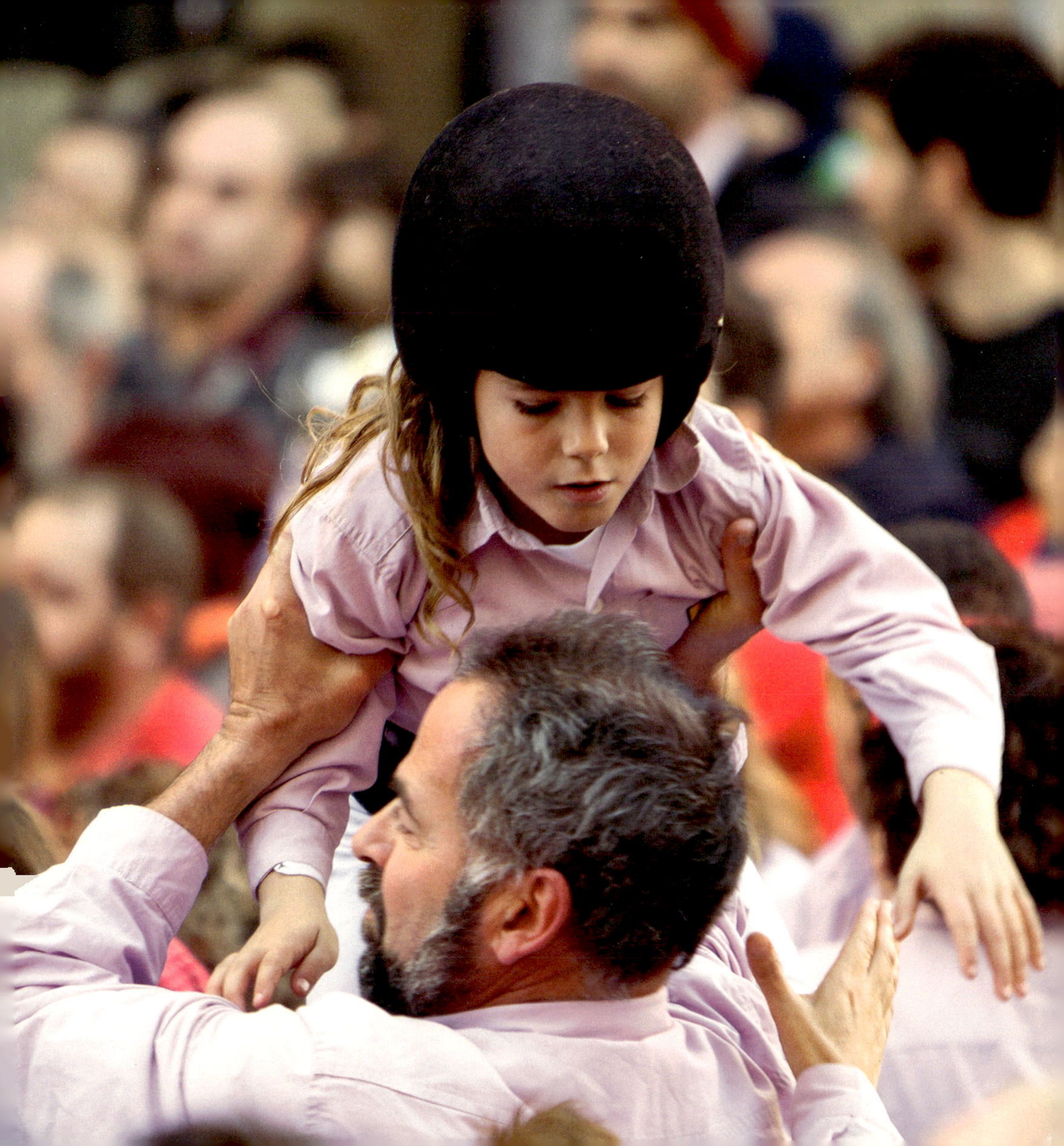

**3.** The *castellers*

Castellers del Poble Sec

# The woman *castellera*

The participation of women in the *castells* is as determinant and essential as that of men. Today no-one could argue with this, and no *colla* is without women. It has not always been like this, because until the 1980s, for a woman to climb up a *castell* was more anecdotal and circumstantial. In short, the *castells* were a man's world. The new generations of *castellers*, however, are committed to eradicating this historical anomaly and make the most of the potential of women who, in many *castells* of many *colles*, situated mainly on the upper storeys, are a fundamental part. There are now several *colles* that are or have been led by women. In the *castells*, the mental capacity of women to resist an effort often surpasses that of men. Moreover, for some specific positions, women have physical advantages over men: with the same size, generally a woman's weight is less than a man's, making their physique more suitable for occupying the high parts of a *castell*.

*Cap de colla* climbing the *castell*. Colla Joves Xiquets de Valls

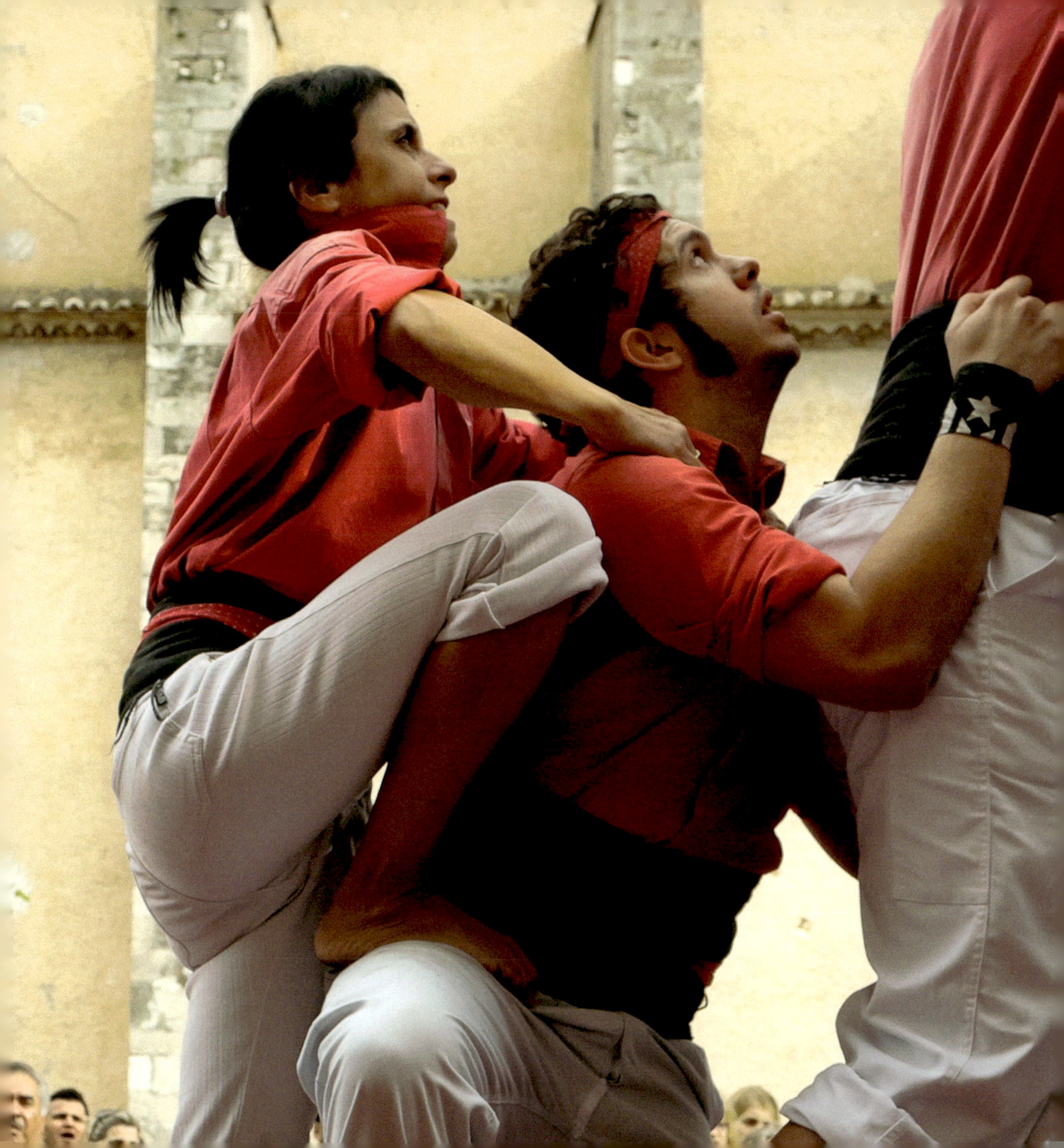

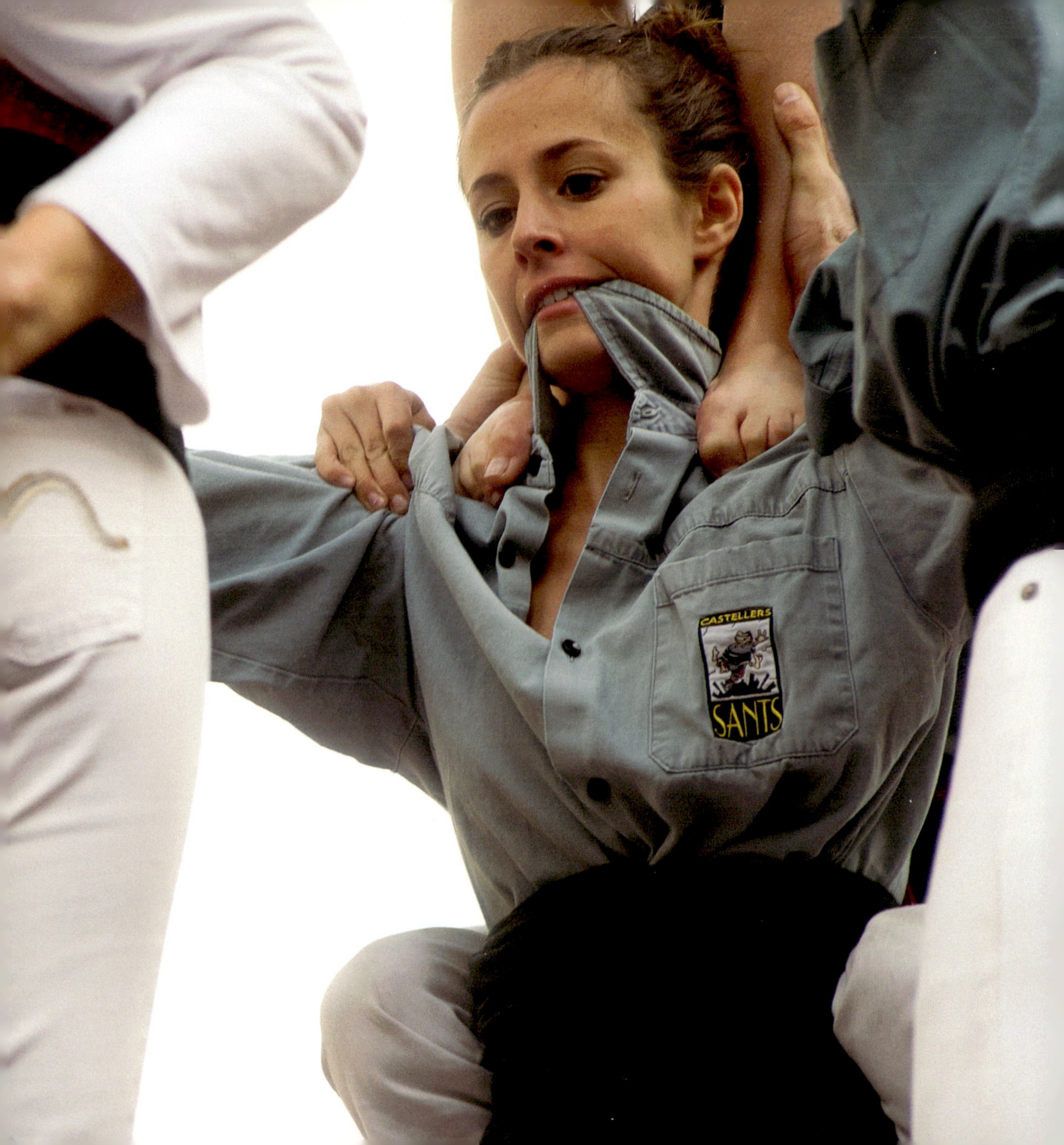
CASTELLERS
SANTS

Minyons de Terrassa. One of the first *colles* that was committed to the participation of women in the *tronc* of the *castells*

Castellers de Sants

**3.** The *castellers*

# The kit or clothing of the *casteller*

Basically, the essential kit of a *casteller* comprises trousers, which are always white and of a resistant fabric, the shirt, also resistant and coloured according to each *colla*, the headscarf, which is traditionally red with white dots, and the waistband, made of cotton and black, which is wrapped around the waist and may be more than 5 metres long and half a metre wide. Among other things, the waistband provides consistency to the body of the *casteller* and aids climbing. Both the shirt and the trousers must be of a fabric that ensures a maximum of adherence, to avoid slipping that could end in a fall. *Castells* are never made in the rain, precisely because it would be easier to slip. The headscarf soaks up the sweat, tied around the waistband stops it from unrolling and, around the thigh, forms a step for the younger ones to climb up on. By the way, on a *castell* you climb up barefoot!

*All the castellers, whatever the position they occupy in a castell, wear a sash*

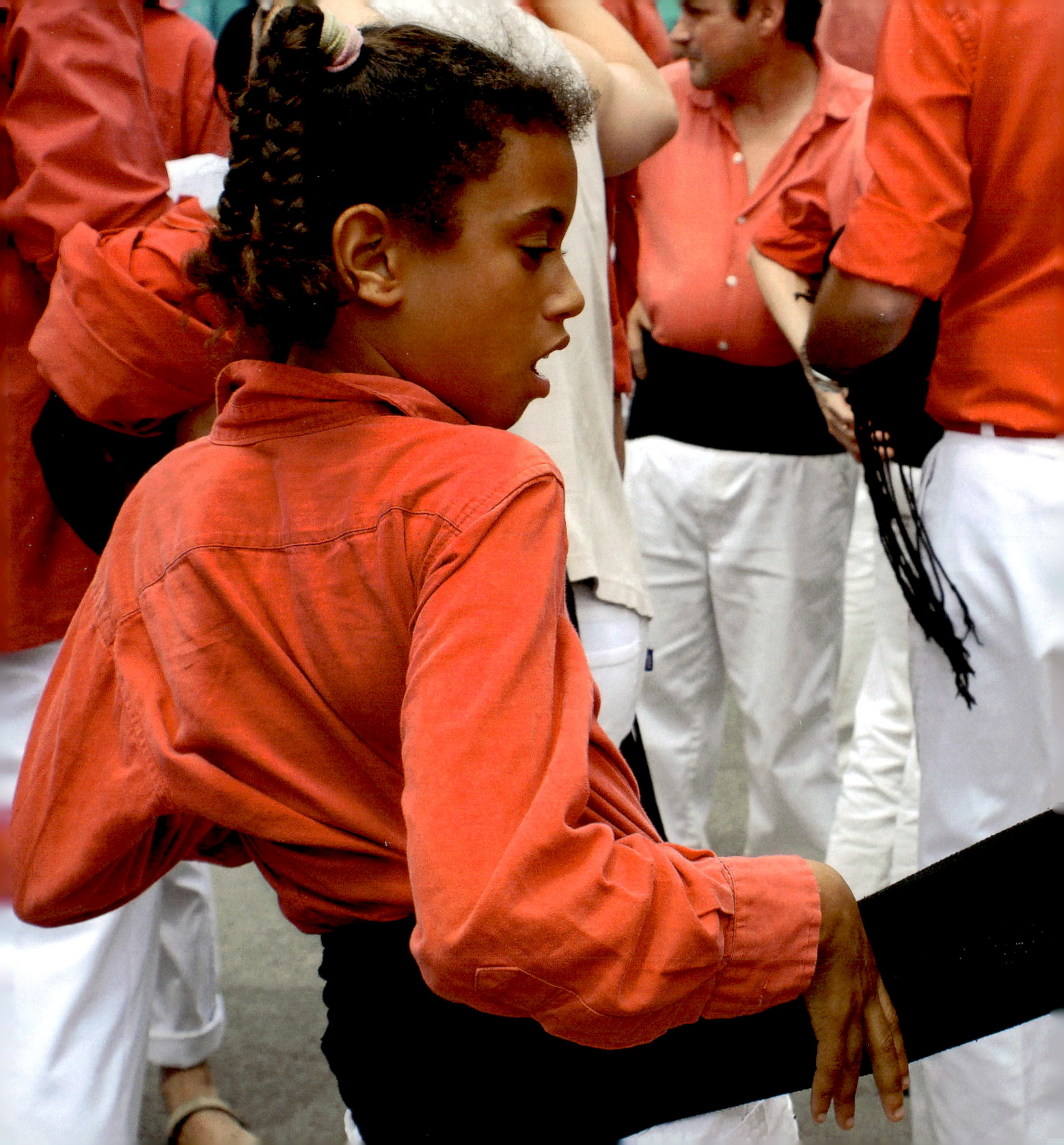

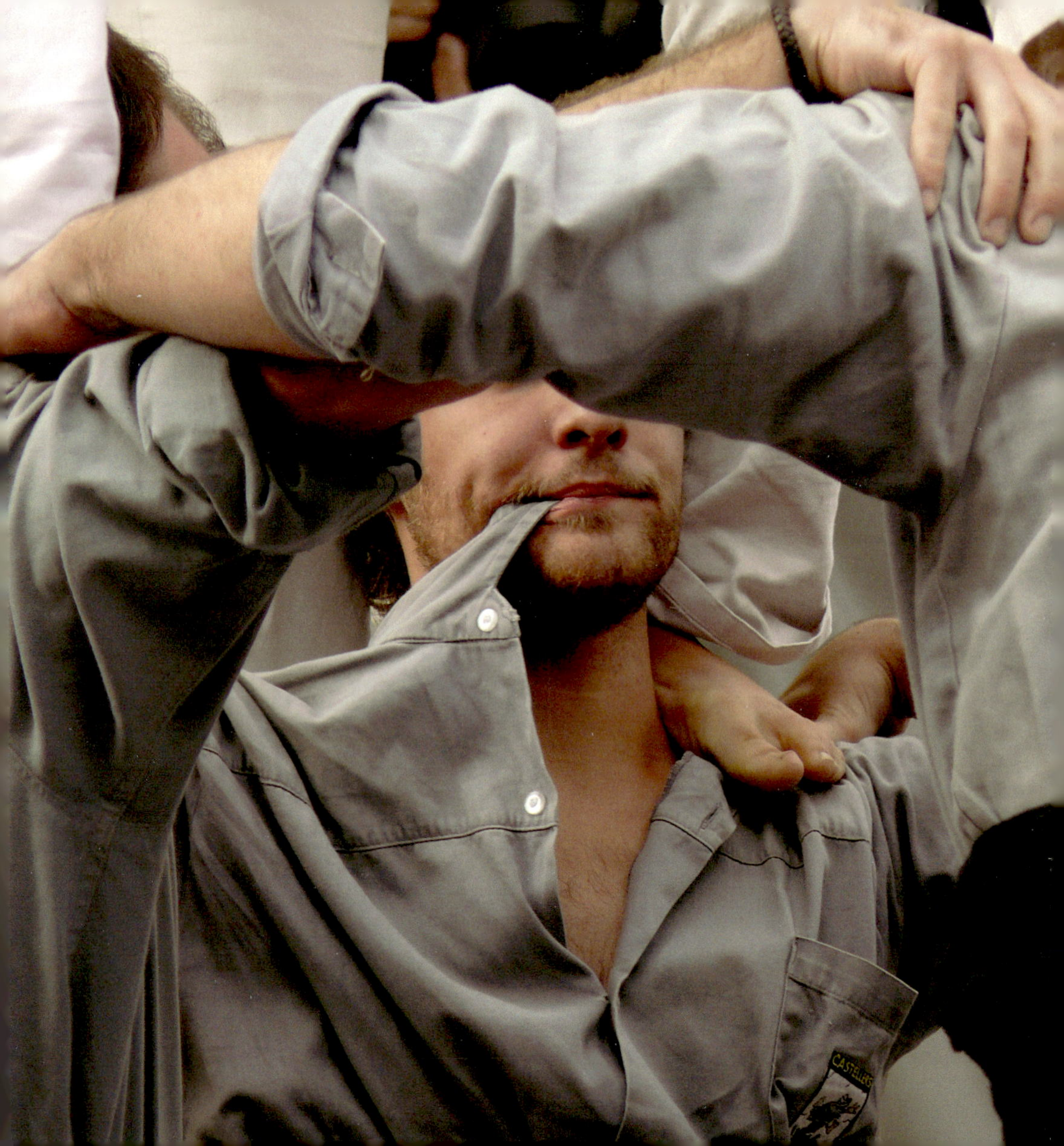
CASTELLERS

# 3. The *castellers*

Many *castellers* wear a headscarf. This practice lies midway between tradition and effectiveness, because it avoids the drops of sweat from running down their faces. Some *castellers* use more than one headscarf: on the wrist, on the sash or on the leg

The *castellers* of the *tronc*, on occasions, bite the collar of the shirt before climbing up them to tighten them and avoid bothersome folds

Generally, the *castellers* need the help of a companion to put the sash on

**3.** The *castellers*

**3.** The *castellers*

# Safety

The first element of safety of a *castell* is the *pinya*, which avoids a *casteller* falling to the ground. The waistband is another, and protects the *casteller's* torso. However, modernisation of the *casteller* world has meant an increase in these measures, with the aim of avoiding injuries. Today, the *castellers* of the higher storeys wear a helmet, and some have a protective mouthpiece. Moreover, in rehearsals there are *castells* that practice surrounded by a net and, on the ground an absorbent element is placed. Safety in *casteller* activity is constantly evolving, the result of several studies led by specialists in medicine.

Minyons de Terrassa

Bordegassos de Vilanova

Colla Jove Xiquets de Tarragona

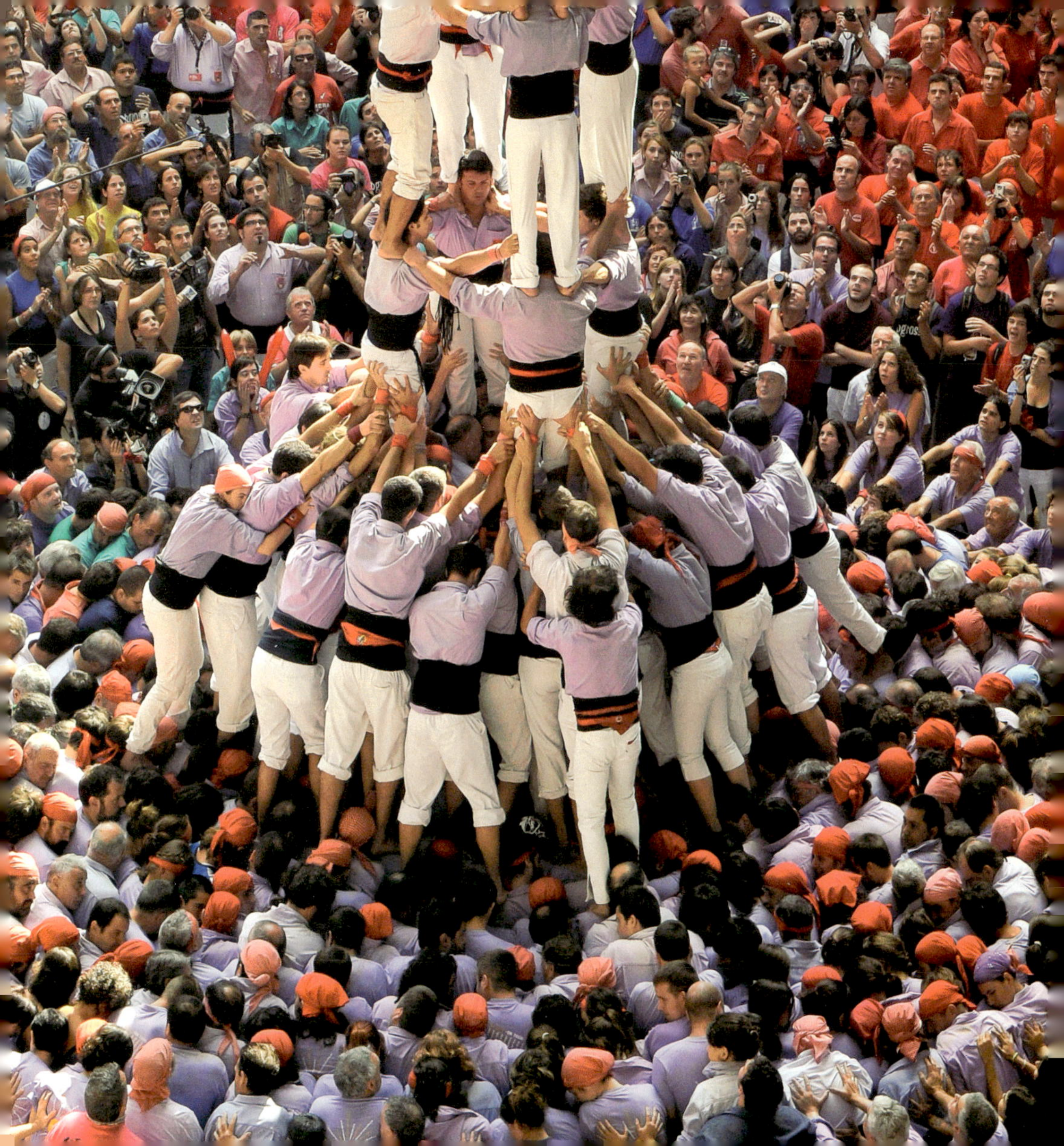

Castellers d'Altafulla

Castellers de Vilafranca

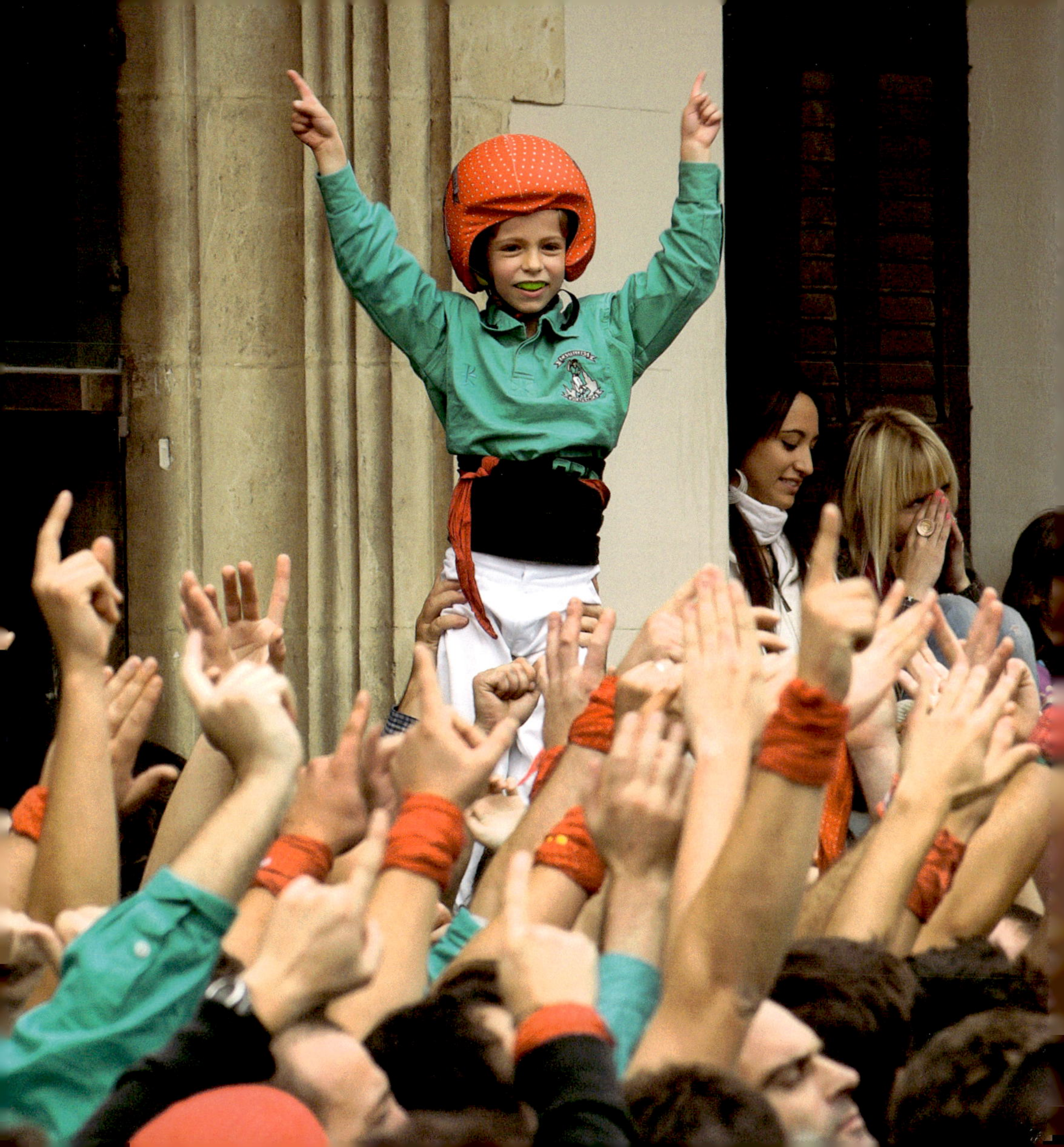

Pom de dalt
Tronc
Manilles
Folre
Pinya

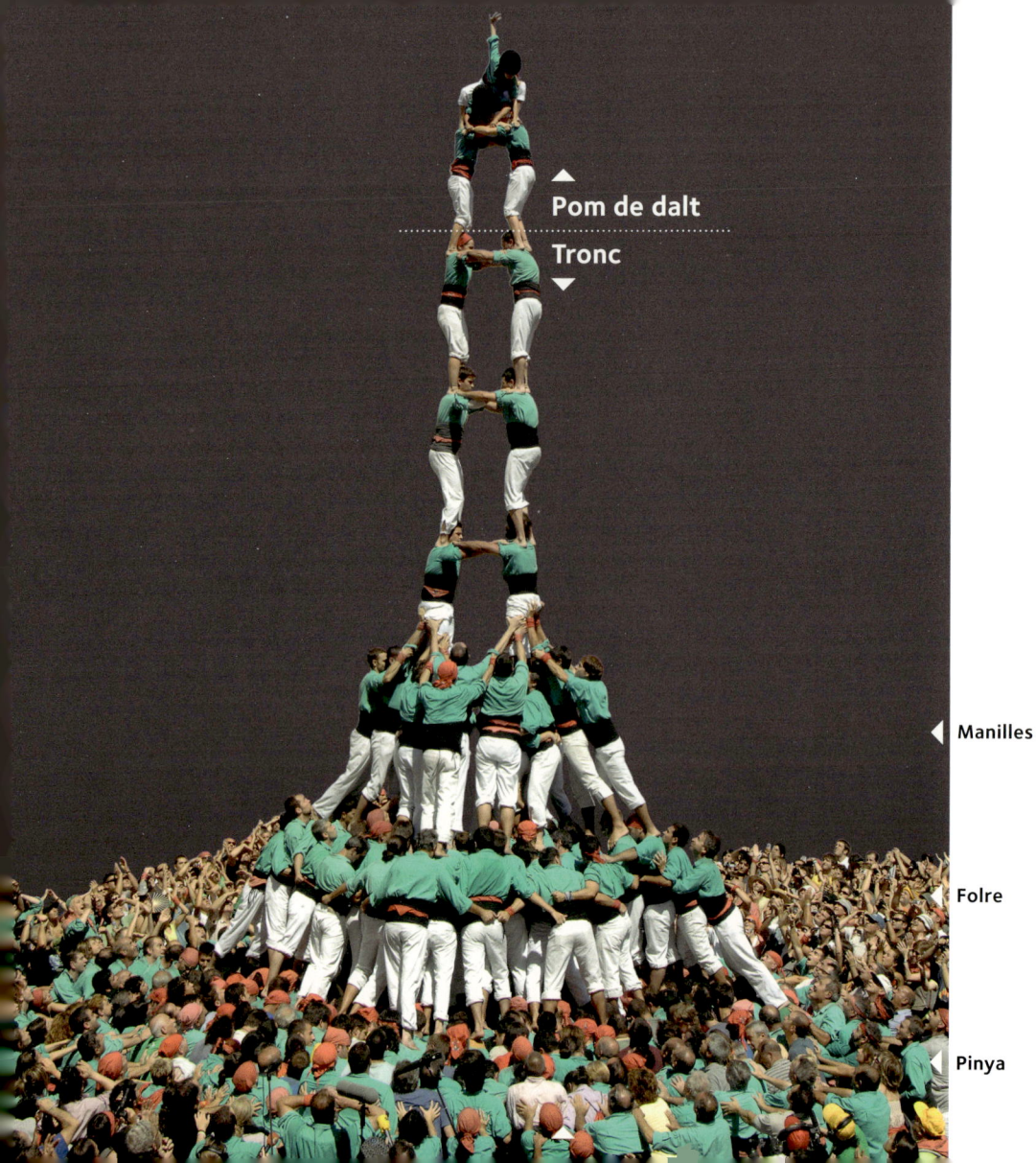

# 4. The parts of a *castell*

At first sight, we can already sense the complexity of the construction of a *castell*. This complexity often increases when we see it adding storeys and the base must be strengthened with new structures. It is true that a human tower, a *castell*, is a whole, a unit. However, it is also formed by semi-independent structures that function interrelating, and which interact from the beginning to the end. For a *castell* to be a success, each of its parts must provide a minimum guarantee of functioning. That is why the *colles* rehearse the *castells* in parts and as a whole. If we look at a *castell* from bottom to top, first we see the *pinya*, and over this two more can be built, the first is called the *folre* and the second, *manilles*. Above these strengthening structures emerges the *tronc* and, above this, at the peak of the *castell*, is the *pom de dalt*. A *castell* can also have more than one *tronc* when its structure is combined, which makes the construction of the *pinya* or the *folre* more complex.

**4.** The parts of a *castell*

# The *pinya*

It is the structure (the foundations) that, situated on the ground, gives consistency to the rest of the *castell* and, in the case of collapse, absorbs the blow. They can be made up of hundreds of *castellers*, placed in an ordered and pre-established form, and each one with a specific function. The *pinya* is the most complex element to produce in a *castell*, especially in its nucleus, where there are *castellers* that must pack out the lower storey and support the second storey of the *castell*. Often, the good state of the *colla* can be measured taking into account the effectiveness and size of the *pinyes* that it can form. It is also the only place where the *colles*, especially if they are not rivals, often collaborate, providing *castellers*.

*Pinya of a castell of 3. Colla Jove Xiquets de Tarragona*

*Pinya of a castell of 2. Castellers de Barcelona*

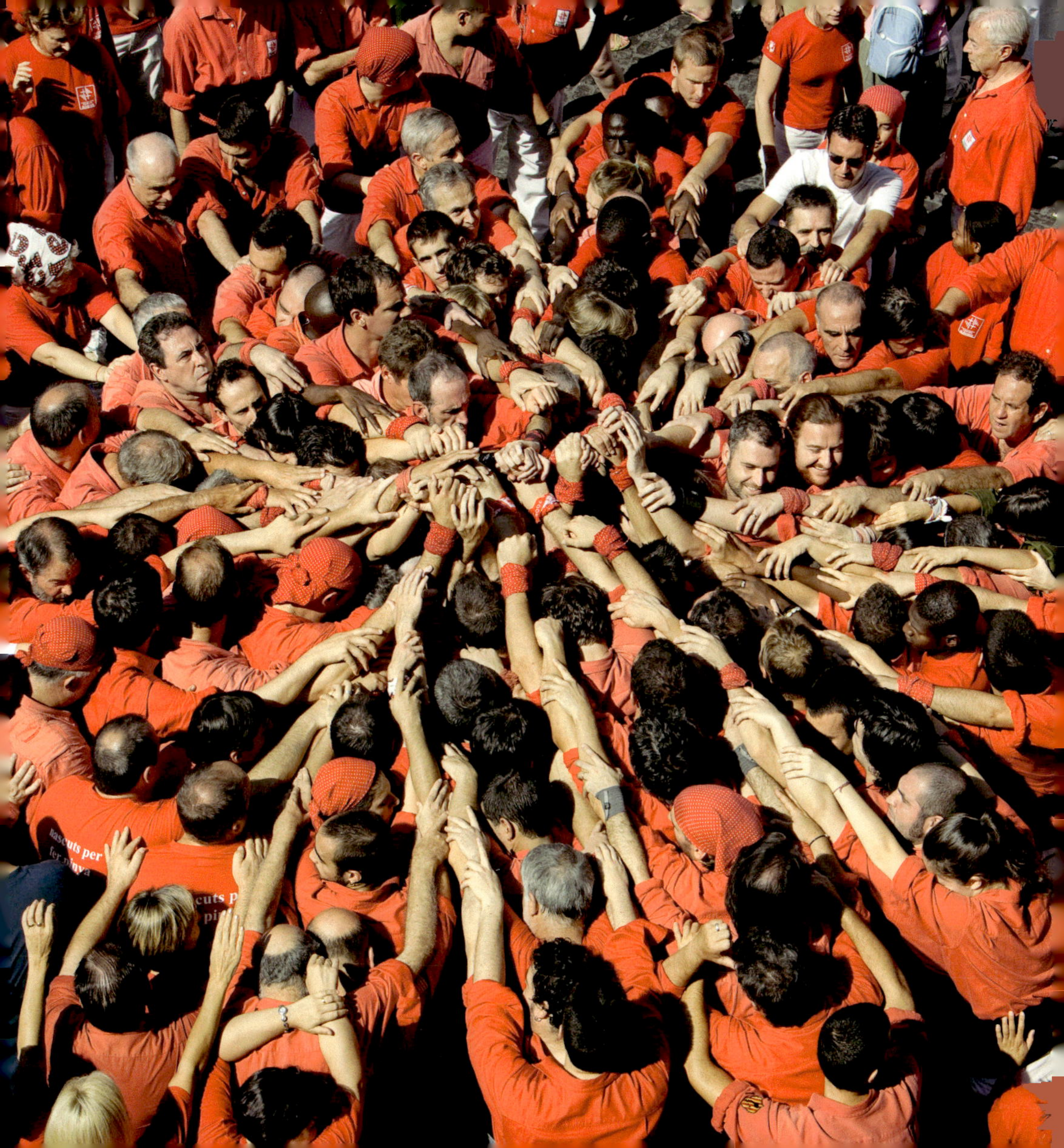
nascuts per
fer pinya

**4.** The parts of a *castell*

# The *castellers* of the *pinya*

In the *castells* there are places, especially in the *pinya*, and also in the *folre* and the *manilles*, which are very demanding and require true specialists. We would highlight the role of the *crosses* (crutches), who fit their shoulders into the armpits of the *baix* of the *tronc* to avoid it collapsing. Also important are the *agulles* (points), situated in the centre of the *castell* and who avoid the members on the ground from moving forward, while they support the knees of the seconds with their hands. There are also the *vents* (winds) and the *laterals* (laterals), which help ensure the *castell* does not distort sideways, and the *primeres mans* (first hands), which support the seconds by their backsides to avoid them sitting. Equally important is the position of the *contrafort* (buttress) or back men, who ensure the members of the ground do not have back strain. These key positions can be repeated in the upper structures of the *folre* and the *manilles*. It is also true, however, that in the *pinya* there is space for everyone with a minimum of physical conditions and the willingness to create a compact whole of human beings.

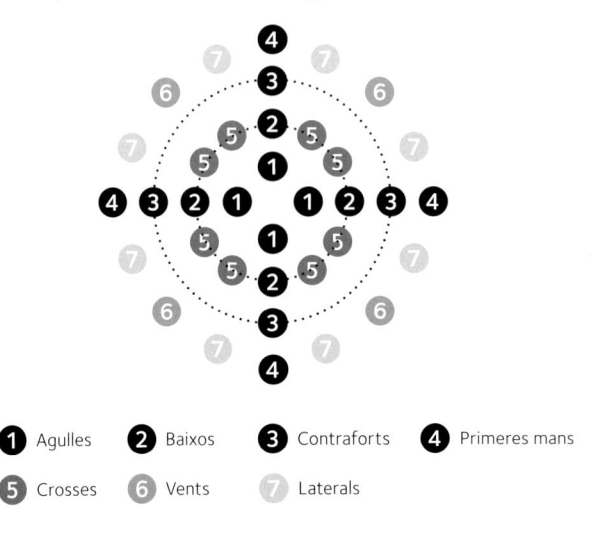

**1** Agulles    **2** Baixos    **3** Contraforts    **4** Primeres mans
**5** Crosses    **6** Vents    **7** Laterals

*Pinya de un castell of 4. Xiquets de Tarragona. In the centre, the 4 agulles, in front of them, the 4 baixos, and behind, the contraforts or back men*

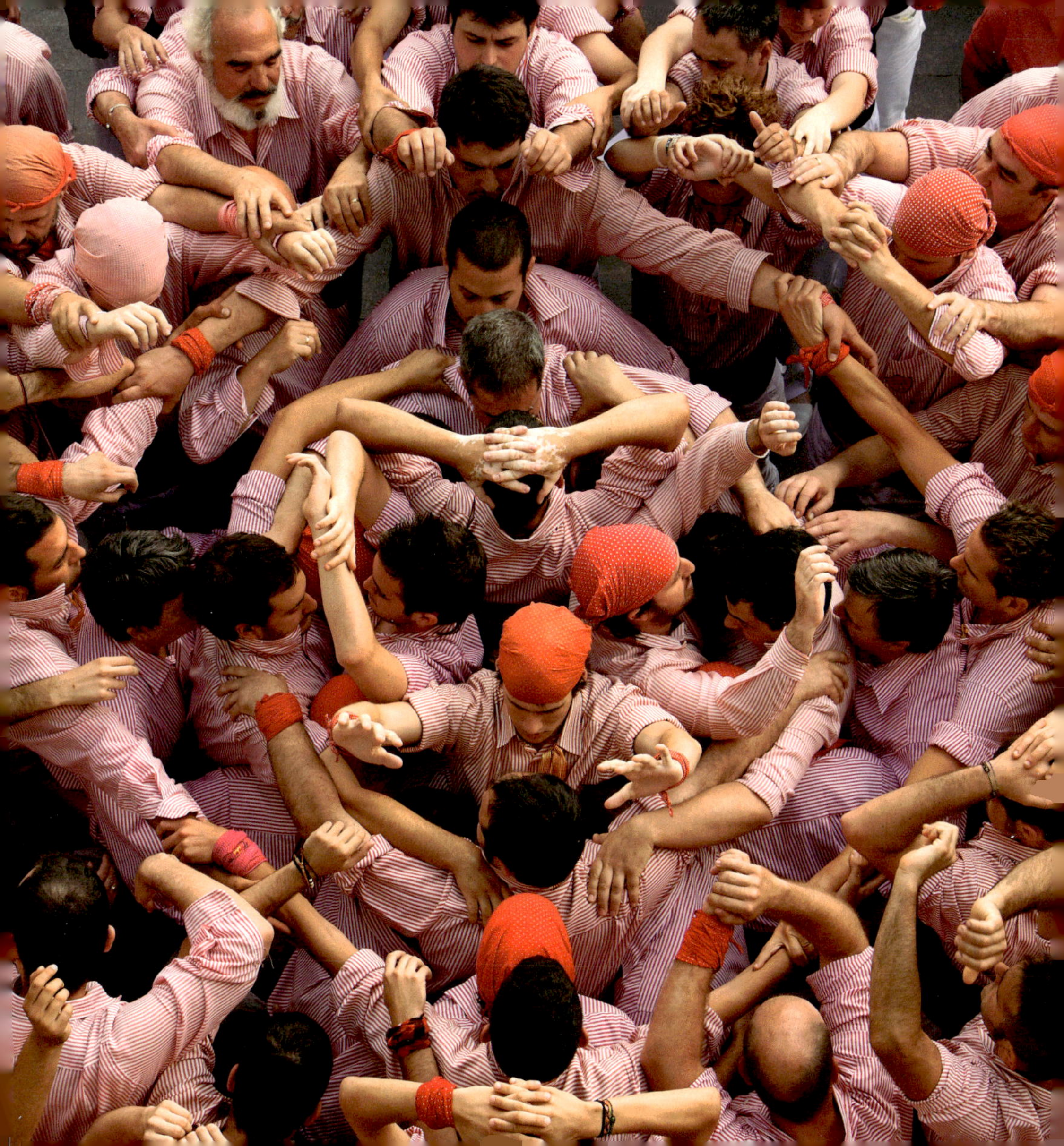

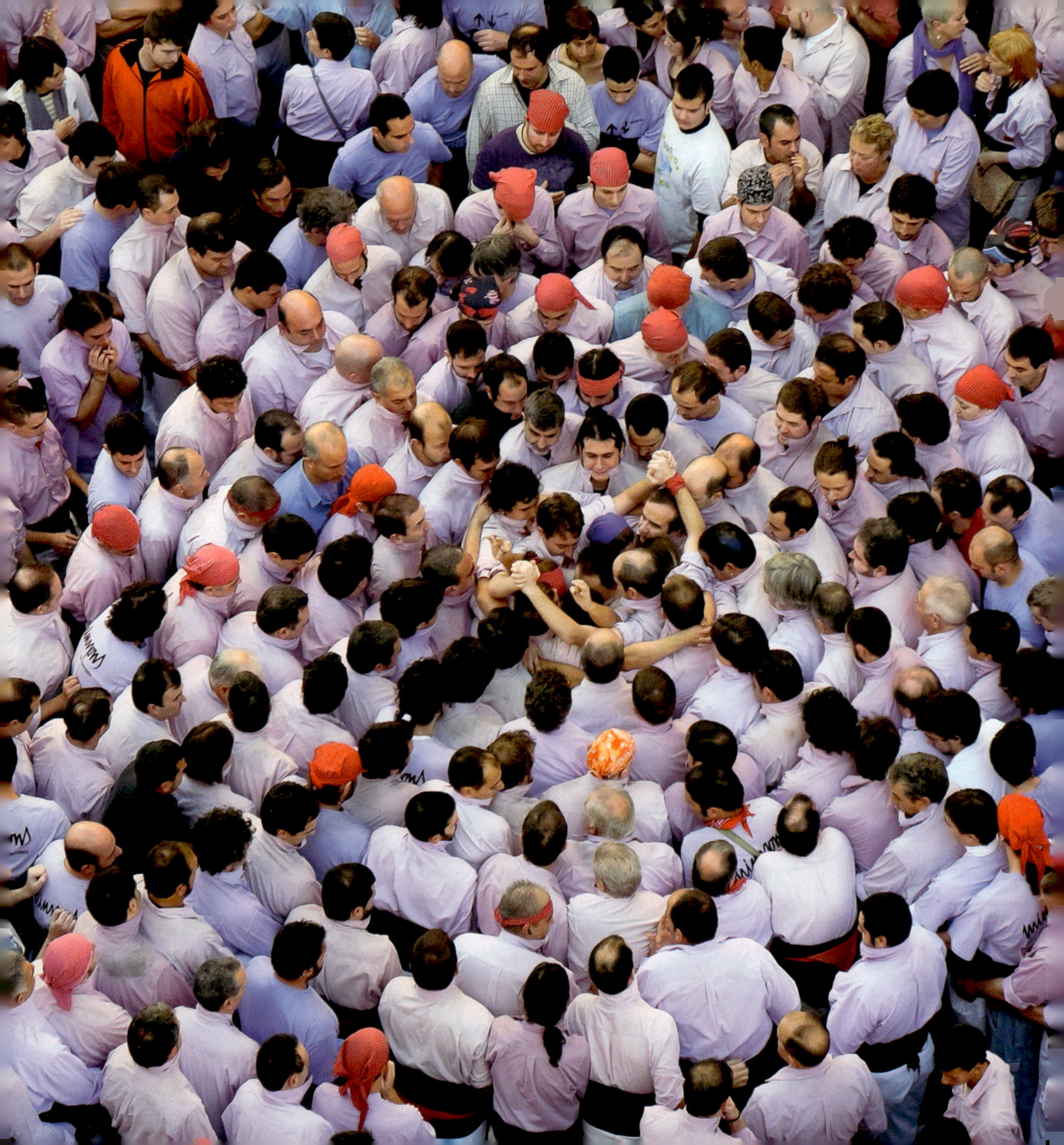

**4.** The parts of a *castell*

*Pinya* of the Minyons de Terrassa

The head of the *pinyes* always has a sketch at hand with the name of the *castellers* and the place that each one of them will occupy in it

95

*Pinya of the Xiquets de Tarragona*

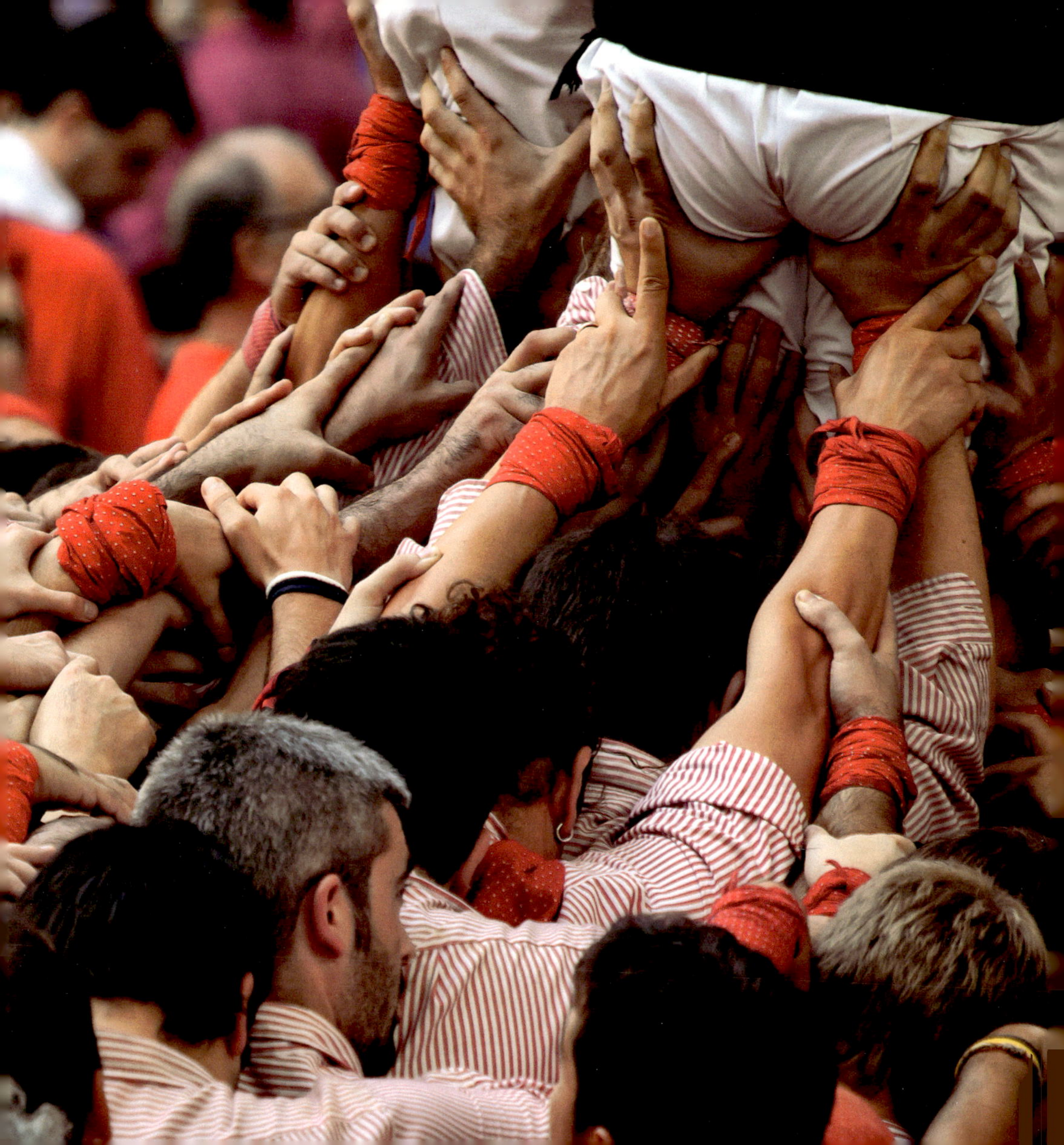

**4.** The parts of a *castell*

# The *tronc*

It is the central structure of the *castell*. It begins on the ground surrounded by the *pinya*. It is made up of several storeys with the same number of *castellers*, and can grow to a maximum height of seven storeys or crowns. There are simple *troncs*, such as the *castell* of 4 or 3 people per storey, and compounds or combined ones, such as that of 5, made up of structures of 3 and 2 *castellers* per storey. The position that the *castellers* occupy (men and women) in the *tronc* depends on their weight, their capacity for physical and mental resistance, their height and the length of their arms. The physical size of the *castellers* gradually decreases as they occupy the higher storeys. Each storey of the *tronc*, and the *castellers* who occupy it, has a name. Thus, the storey that touches the ground is the *baixos* (ground) and each *casteller* that forms it is called *baix*. The second storey is *segons* (seconds), and a *casteller* who occupies this places is a *segon*. The third storey is the *terços* (thirds), the fourth *quarts* (fourths), the fifth, *quints* (fifths), the sixth storey is known as *sisens* (sixths) and the seventh, *setens* (sevenths).

*Tronc of the 4 of 8 _ Castellers de Barcelona*

**4.** The parts of a *castell*

Minyons de Terrassa

Colla Joves Xiquets de Valls

Colla Vella dels Xiquets de Valls

Interior view of the *tronc* and the *pom de dalt* of a 4 of 7. Castellers de Vilafranca

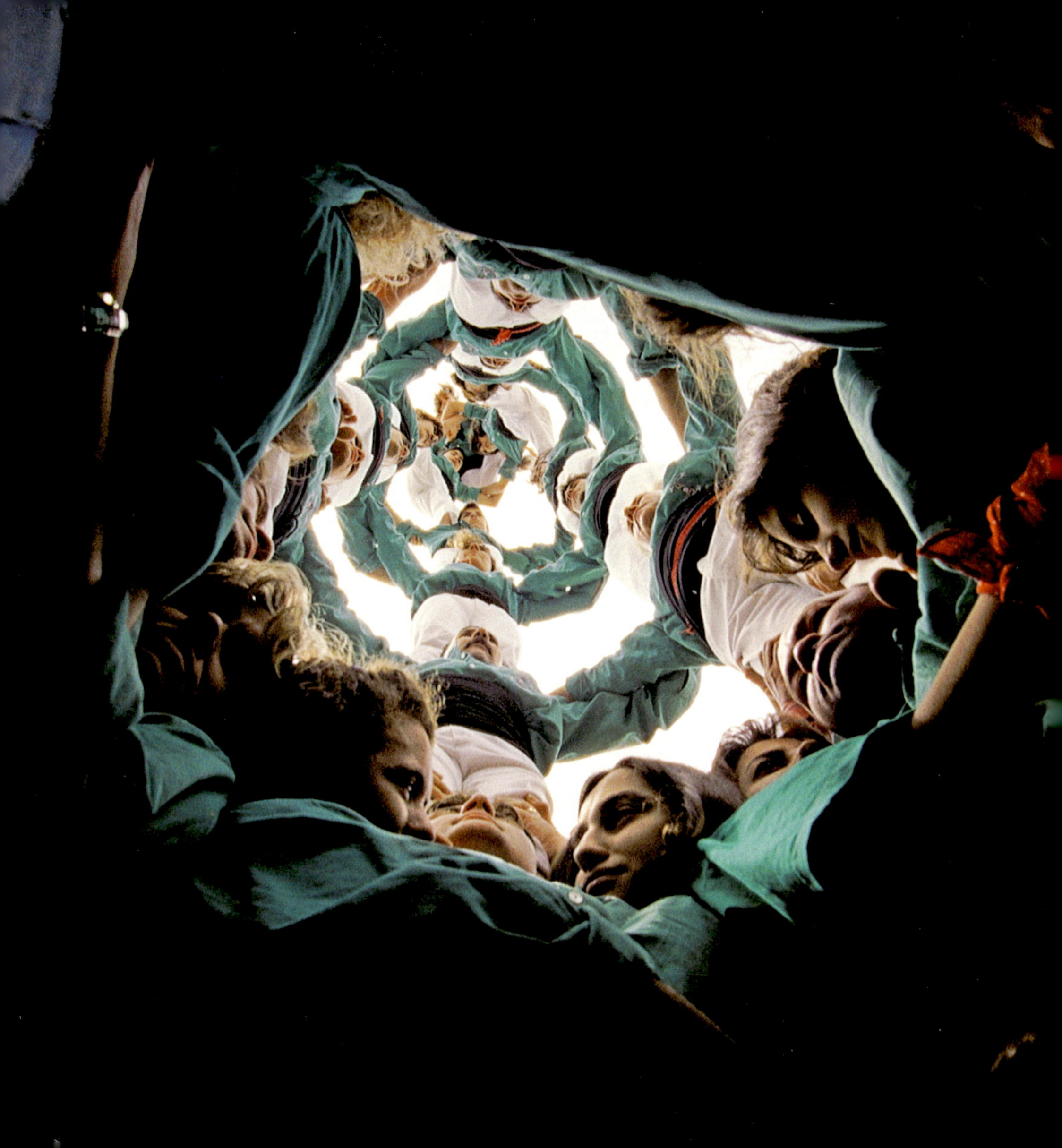

**4.** The parts of a *castell*

# The *pom de dalt*

It is the higher part of a *castell*, formed by the last three storeys, and which is situated at the top of the *tronc*. It is made up of a series of two *castellers* called *dosos* (literally, twos), above which is another storey with just one *casteller*, in this case crouching, who is usually the smallest of a *castell*, called *aixecador*, *acotxador* or *cassoleta*, according to the *colles*, and, above them, the last storey, with another sole *casteller* who, when positioned in their place raises their hand or does the *aleta*. This *casteller* is called *enxaneta*. The four *castellers* that form this structure, and particularly the two latter ones, the *aixecador* and the *enxaneta*, must be extremely delicate and quick when they climb and descend the *castell*. These qualities determine whether the structure suffers from tiredness or brusque movements, which could destabilise it and make it collapse.

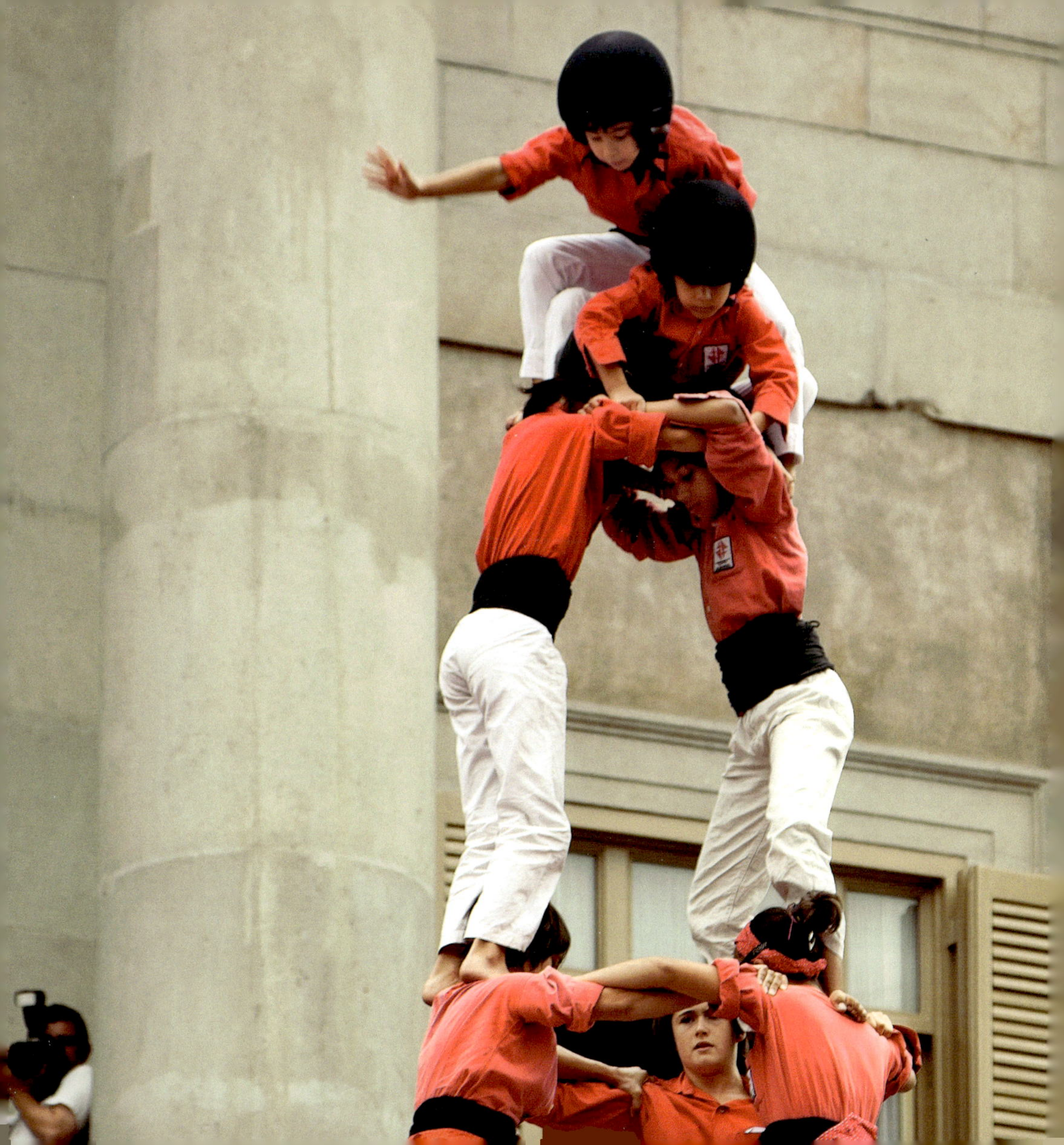

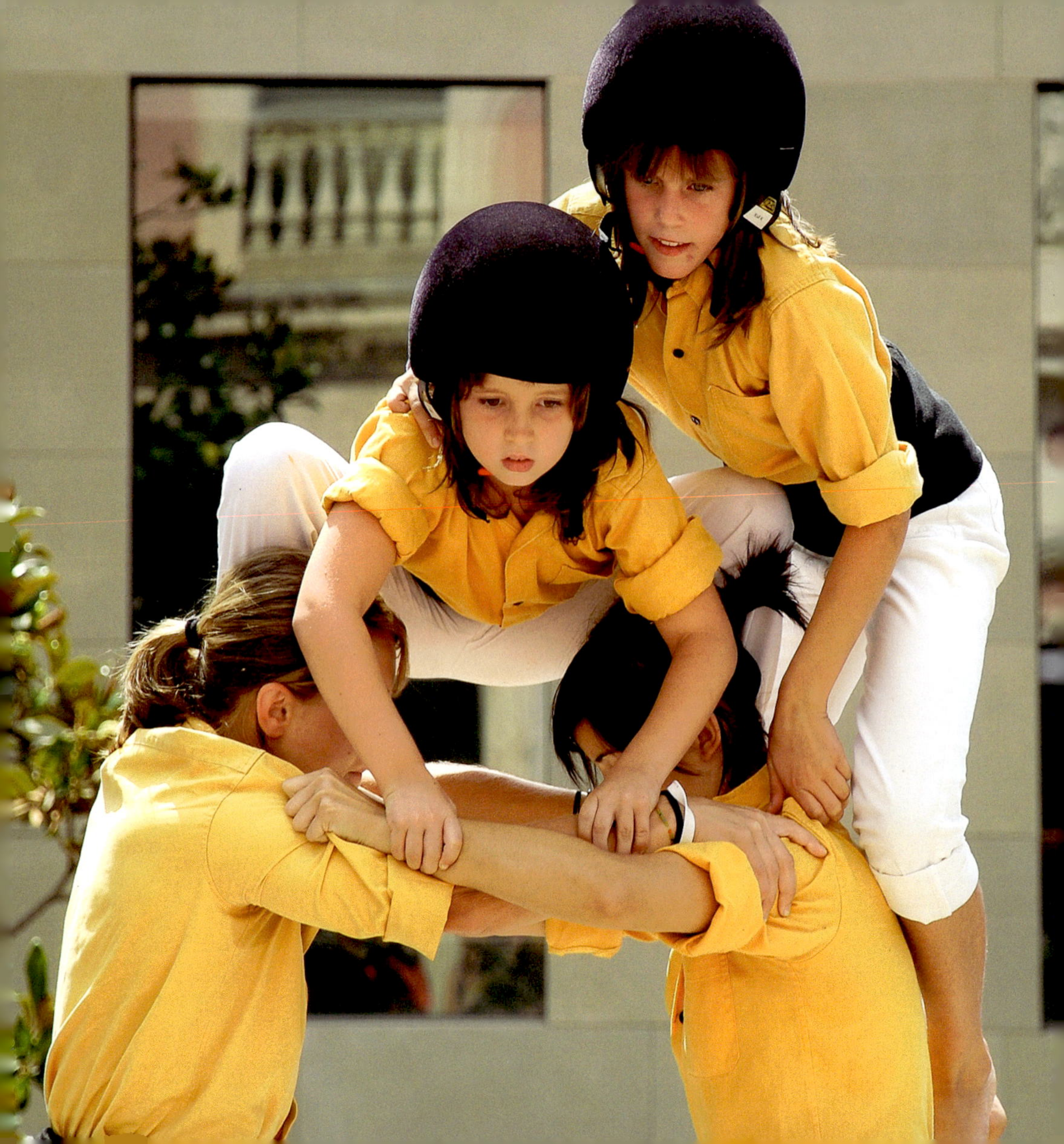

Bordegassos de Vilanova

Xiquets de Tarragona

**4.** The parts of a *castell*

# The *folre*

In more difficult *castells*, over the *pinya* is placed a large number of *castellers*, who strengthen the second storey of the *castell* and hold the third storey with their hands in the form of a buttress. It is like a small *pinya*, which is called *folre*. Generally it is assembled in *castells* of nine storeys, but also in the *torre* of eight with *folre* and in *pilar* of seven with *folre*. Unlike the *pinya*, the *castellers* of the *folre* must endeavour not to push forward with their chests, but rather apply the greater part of their effort in giving consistency to the higher storey of *terços*.

Castellers de Vilafranca

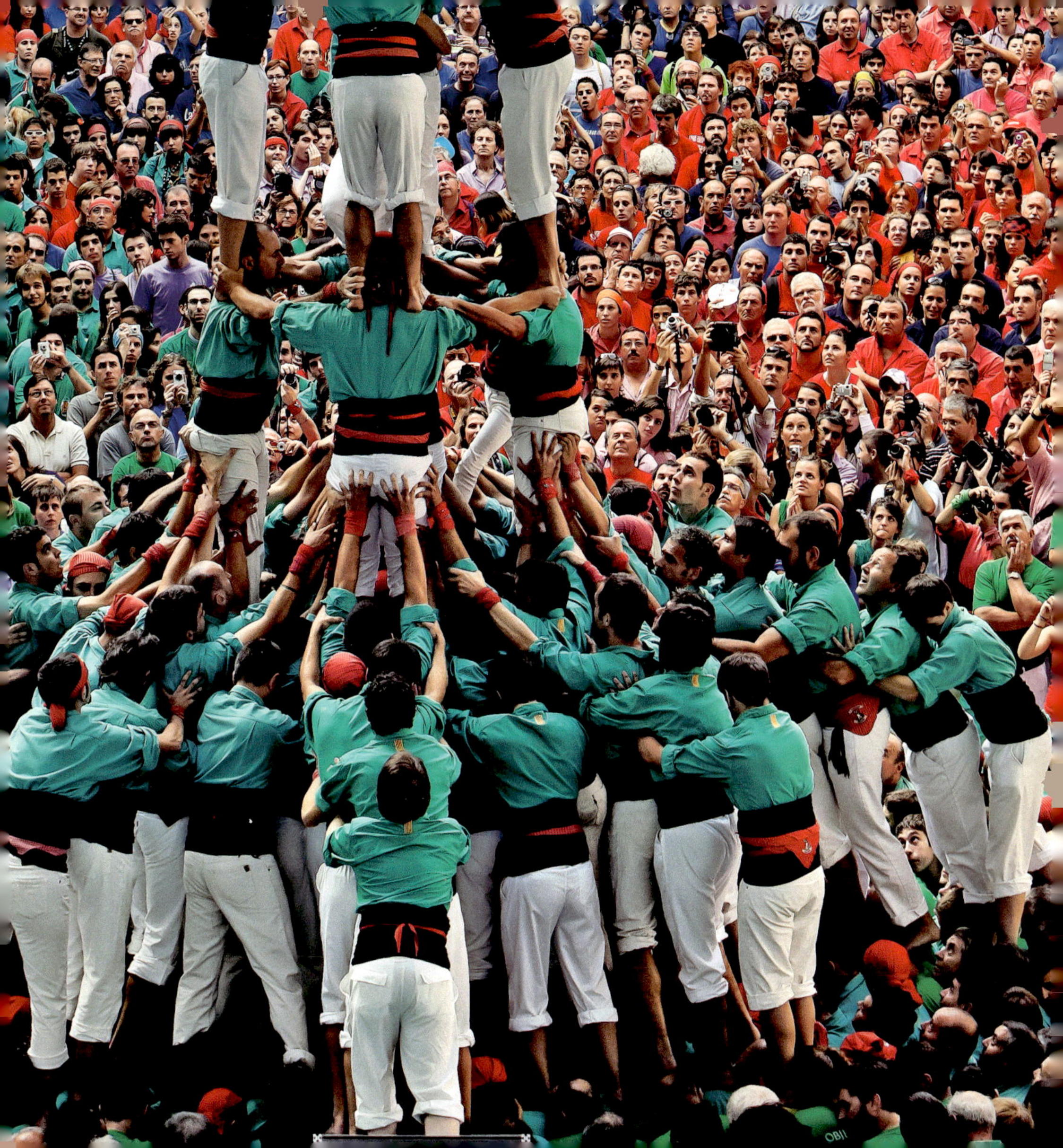

**4.** The parts of a *castell*

# The *manilles*

In very difficult *castells*, also called *Gama Extra*, the strengthening or *folre* over the *pinya* is not enough. Another group of *castellers* is needed that climbs above the *folre*, to give consistency to the third storey and holds the storey of *quarts* with their hands. This third strengthening is called *manilles*. It is used, for example, in the *tres* of ten with *folre* and *manilles*, and also in the *pilar* of eight with *folre* and *manilles* and in the *dos*, or *torre*, of nine with *folre* and *manilles*. Over the *manilles* another supra-structure can still be built, called *puntals*. It would be placed in a hypothetical *pilar* of nine with *folre*, *manilles* and *puntals*. This *castell* has been rehearsed by the Castellers de Vilafranca group.

Minyons de Terrassa

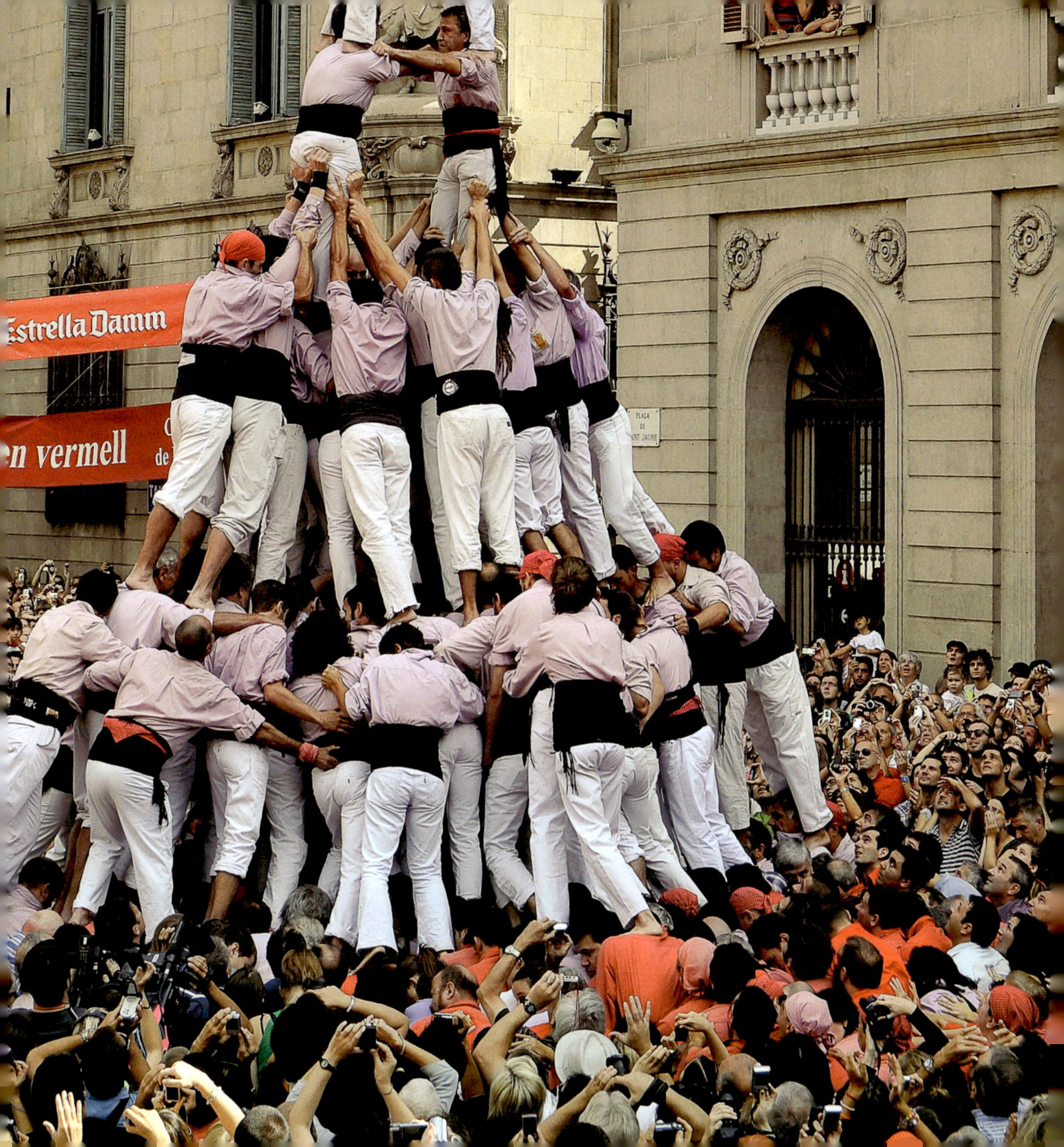
Estrella Damm
en vermell

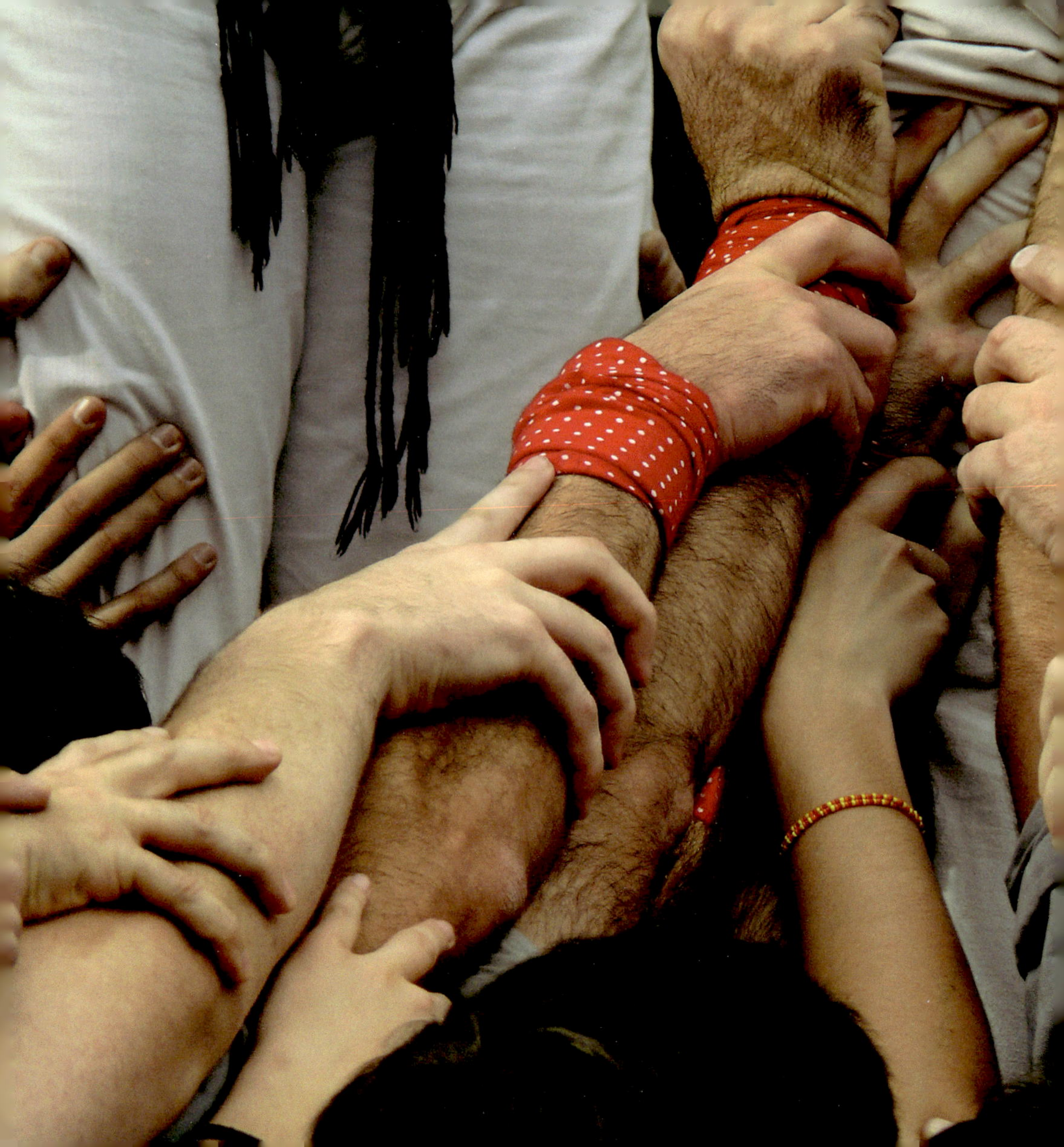

# 5. All the *castells*

As you can see, the *castells* are built with people who climb on top of each other to a maximum height of ten storeys, in the best of cases. Each *castell* has a name and, nearly always, is determined by two parameters: the number of *castellers* per storey and the number of storeys it has, always in this order, never the other way round. Therefore a *castell* where there are three *castellers* and which has eight storeys in height is called *tres de vuit* (three of eight). The *castells* that have only one *casteller* per storey are called *pilar* (pillar), those with two, *torre* or *dos* (tower or two), those with three, *tres* (three), those with four, *quatre* (four) and those with five, *cinc* (five). Each number must be followed by the height in storeys, for example: *pilar de sis* (pillar of six). There are also *castells* built with *agulla* (point) or *pilar* in half. Basically there are two, the *quatre amb l'agulla* (four with point) and the *tres amb l'agulla* (three with point). These *castells* are the same as the three or four, but in the centre of the structure a *pilar* is added. In these cases, the *castell* is called, for example if it is of three *castellers* per storey and eight storeys, *tres de vuit amb l'agulla* (three of eight with point).

There are also *castells* that are built with a technique almost in reverse to the regular way of climbing storey to storey: they are the *castells aixecats per sota* (raised from below). In this case the first *castellers* that appear over the *pinya* are the smallest, and which, beneath these, successively, appear storeys of *castellers* rising in weight from below. The most common are the *pilar aixecat per sota* (pillar raised from below) and the three *tres aixecat per sota* (three raised from below). As well as the classics, there are also unusual *castells*, which do not form part of the regular repertoire and which the *colles*

## 5. All the castells

only create in exceptional cases, often as a form of entertainment. Among these feature the *cinc amb agulla* (five with point), a modern invention that the Castellers de Vilafranca have achieved of eight storeys, the *dotze* (twelve), *dos aixecat per sota* (two raised from below), or the *nou* (nine), this latter one with nine *castellers* in each storey, with a structure formed by a central *tres* that has three structures of attached *dos*. This *castell* was built back in the 19th century, but the first *nou* (nine) documented of eight storeys is in this century. The Colla Vella dels Xiquets de Valls achieved it in 2001 with three *enxanetes* who crowned each of the three structures of *dos*.

We should be aware that an attempt to build a *castell* begins when, according to the height it will be, the music begins to play and not before. In fact, the construction of the base or *pinya* and of the structures of *folre* and *manilles* can be considered an introduction, a vital one indeed, but only an introduction. We should also know that a *castell* is finished, or considered disassembled, when the very storey of *castellers* that began to form with the music, climbs down to the *pinya* without incidents, although the music continues playing until the *pinya* has been completely disassembled.

The *castells* begin to be assessed as from six storeys, except for the *pilar*, which is considered worthy when it has four storeys.

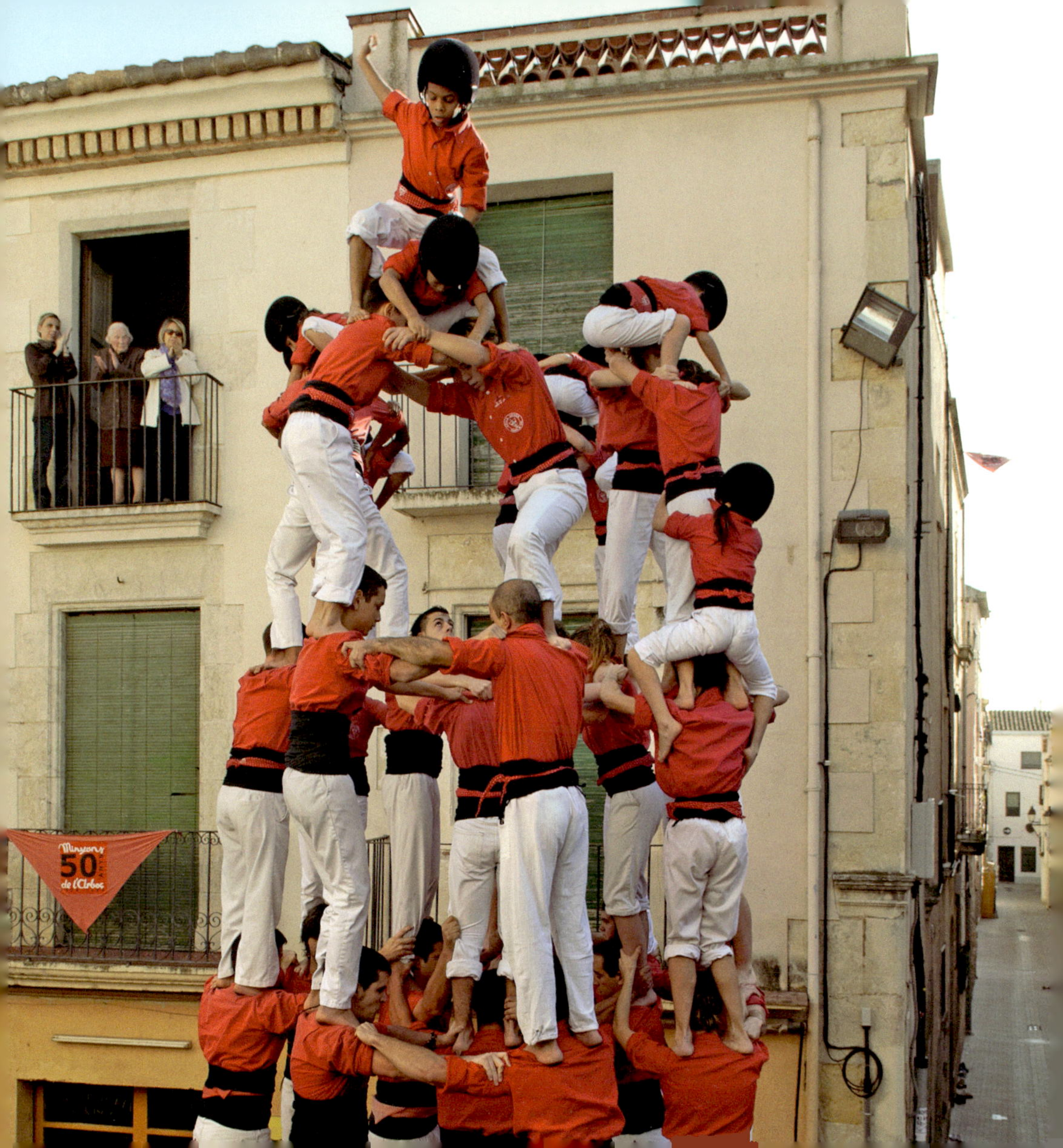
Minyons
50
ANYS
de l'Arboç

**5.** All the *castells*

7 of 7 _ Margeners de Guissona

7 of 7 _ Castellers de Sants

5 of 8 with the point _ Castellers de Vilafranca

**5.** All the *castells*

# El pilar
## The pillar

Construction of one *casteller* per storey which, suitably strengthened, can reach eight storeys in height. This construction was already built in the 19th century by the two *colles* of Valls, and in the 20th century the Castellers de Vilafranca recovered it, building it successfully for the first time in 1995 and managing to build and disassemble it 1997. Generally, the pillars are built to end a performance, but when they surpass five storeys in height, it is not unusual to make them in the middle. Often, in their version of four storeys, the *colles* make the *pinya* walk for several dozen metres or more. They can also be built of five or six storeys, flanked by two pillars from a lower storey. This series of pillars is called *vano de cinc o sis* (fan of five or six), according to the height of the central pillar. As we have mentioned, it can also be built from top to bottom. In this case, the first thing that appears above the *pinya* is the *enxaneta*, who is raised as *castellers* are positioned below, rising in weight. While the *pilar* is a structure of one *casteller* per storey, in the pillars of seven with *folre* and eight with *folre* and *manilles*, the storeys of seconds and of seconds and thirds, respectively, are built with a false structure of two *castellers* per storey to give it more stability.

Pillar of 8 with *folre* and *manilles* _ Colla Vella dels Xiquets de Valls ↓Pillar of 8 with *folre* and *manilles* _ Castellers de Vilafranca

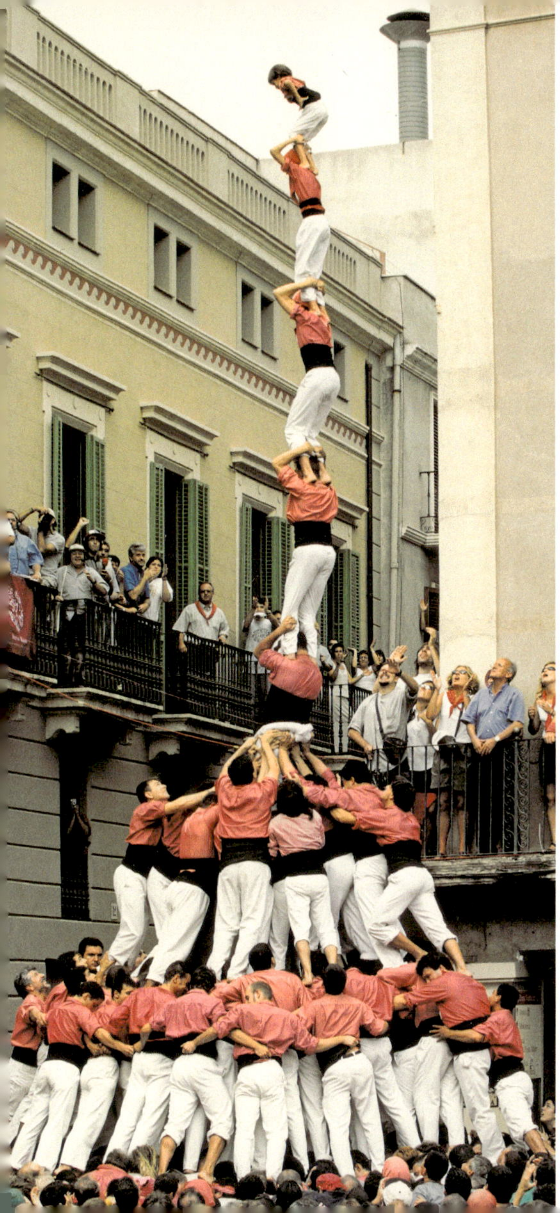
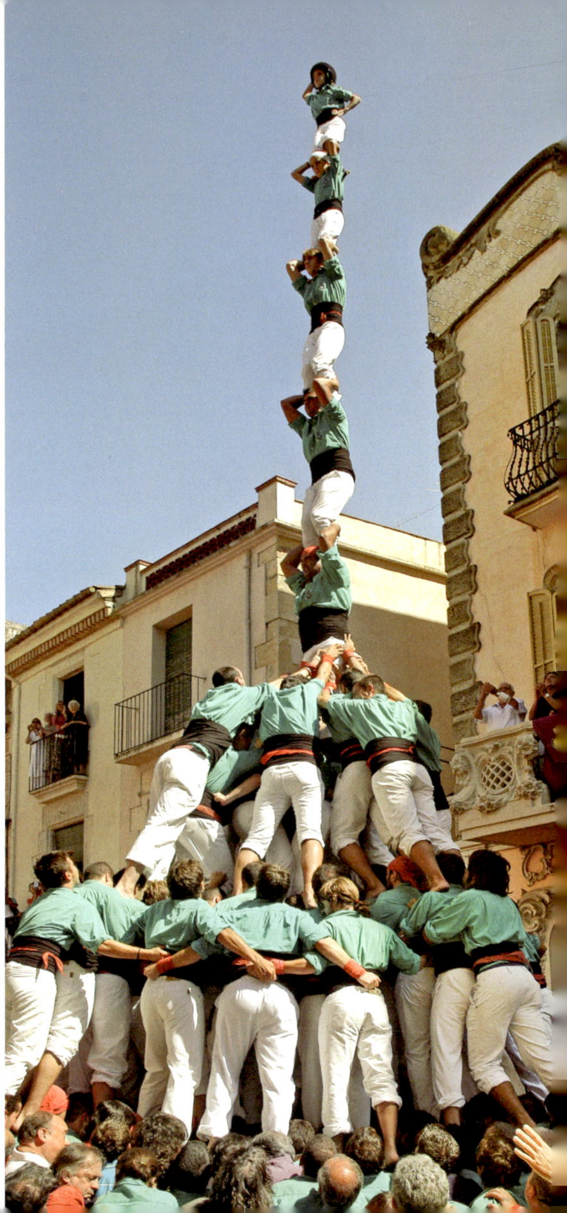

Pillar of 8 with *folre* and *manilles* _ Minyons de Terrassa

**5.** All the *castells*

Pillar of 7 with *folre* _ Castellers de Barcelona

Pillar of 6 _ Xiquets de Tarragona

Pillar of 5 _ Xicots de Vilafranca

Pillar of 5 _ Castellers de Sabadell

Pillar of 5 _ Castellers de Sants        Pillar of 4 walking _ Xerrics d'Olot

**5.** All the *castells*

Pillar of 4 _ Global de Salou

Pillar going down steps _ Castellers de Mollet

Pillar of 4 _ Nois de la Torre

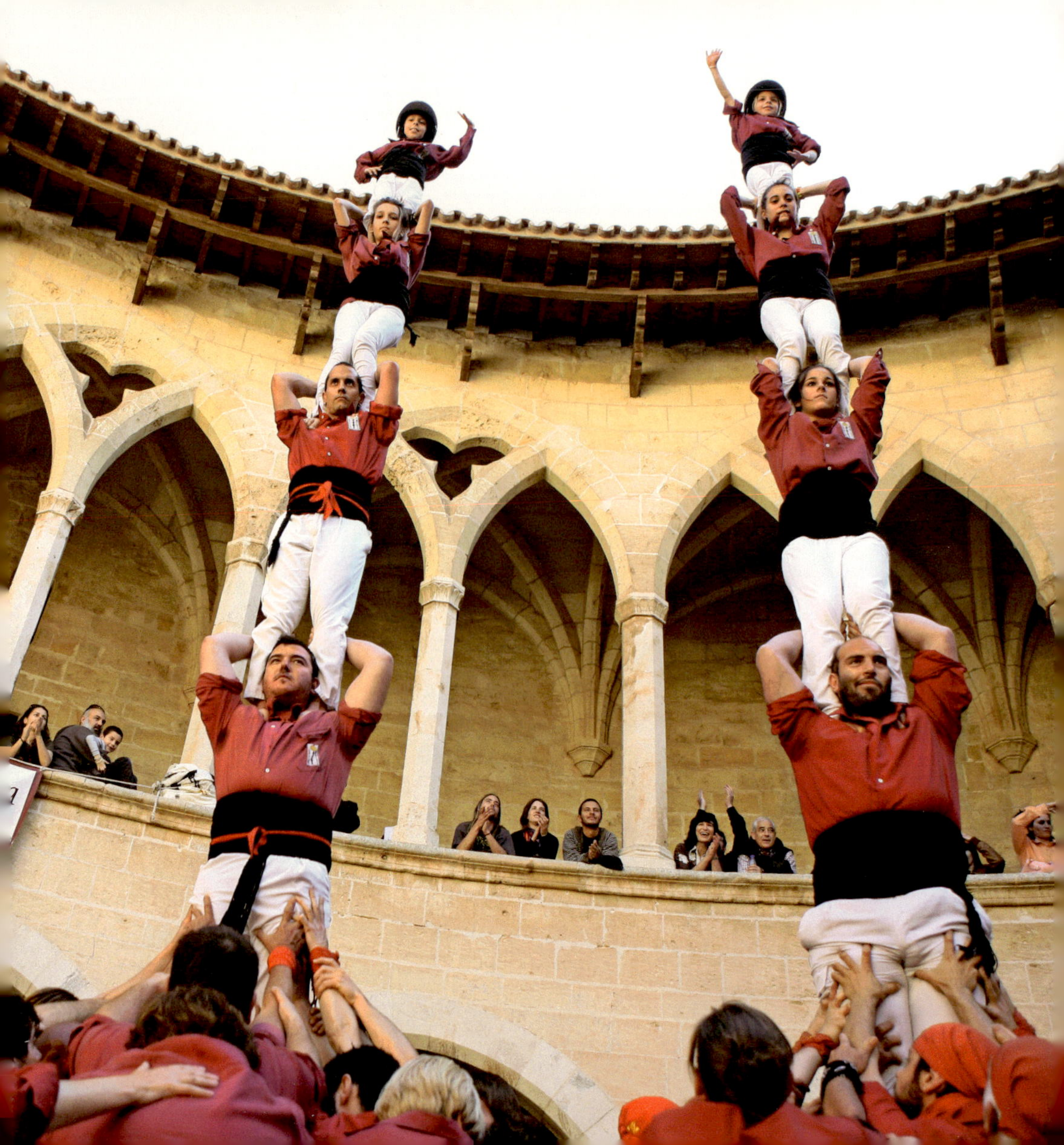

Two Pillars of 5 _ Castellers de Mallorca. Castell de Bellver. Palma

Pillar of 5 on the balcony _ Castellers de Barcelona

Fan of 6 _ Minyons de Terrassa

Pillar of 5 built from below _ Bordegassos de Vilanova

**5.** All the *castells*

◀ **The two or tower**
p. 132

**The three** ▶
p. 144

**5.** All the *castells*

◀ **The four**
p. 156

**The five** ▶
p. 174

**5.** All the *castells*

# El dos o torre
## The two or tower

Construction of two *castellers* per storey which, strengthened at the base, can reach a height of nine storeys. With the *dos*, this height was achieved for the first time ever in 1993, when the Minyons de Terrassa built it. A year later, in 1994, the Colla Vella dels Xiquets de Valls became the first group to build and disassemble it. In the *torre* or *dos* of nine a second strengthening or *manilles* is always placed over the *folre*. However, in 2005, the Castellers de Vilafranca also built it without this second strengthening, which was considered a remarkable feat. This *castell* was called *torre* of nine without *manilles*. Generally, the *dos*, when it has eight storeys, has a strengthening or *folre* above the *pinya*. However, it can also be built without it, although this version, called clear tower of eight, or without *folre*, is extremely difficult. It is so extraordinary that it was not built and disassembled for the first time ever until the 1 November 2010, by the Castellers de Vilafranca. On that day, *castellers* fans who were able to see it were aware that they were witnessing and unique and difficult to repeat feat. The clear two of eight has also been built by the Colla Vella dels Xiquets de Valls and the Colla Joves Xiquets de Valls.

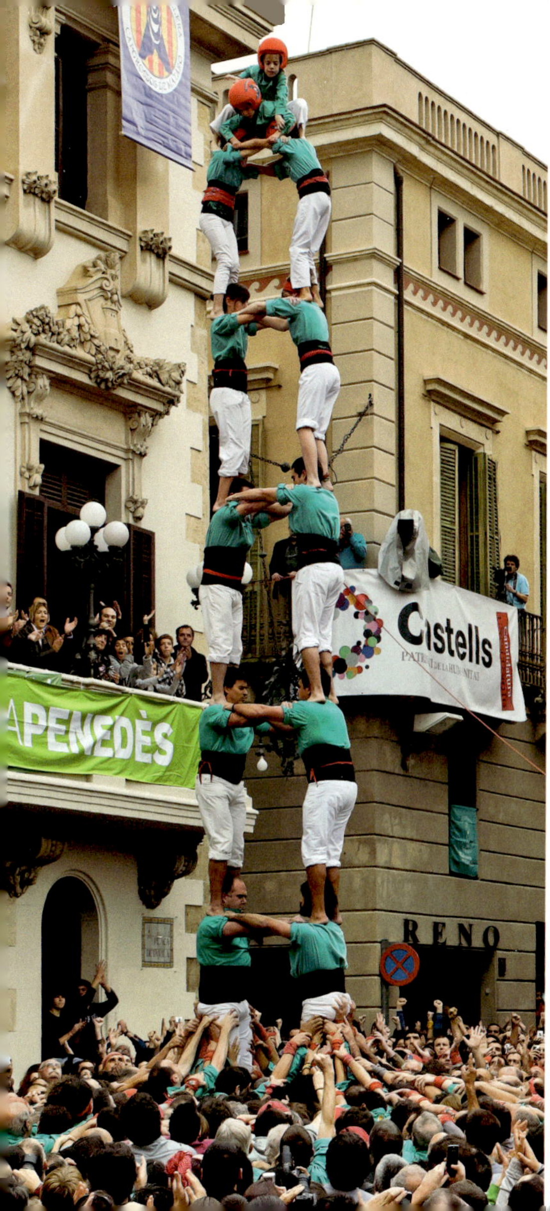

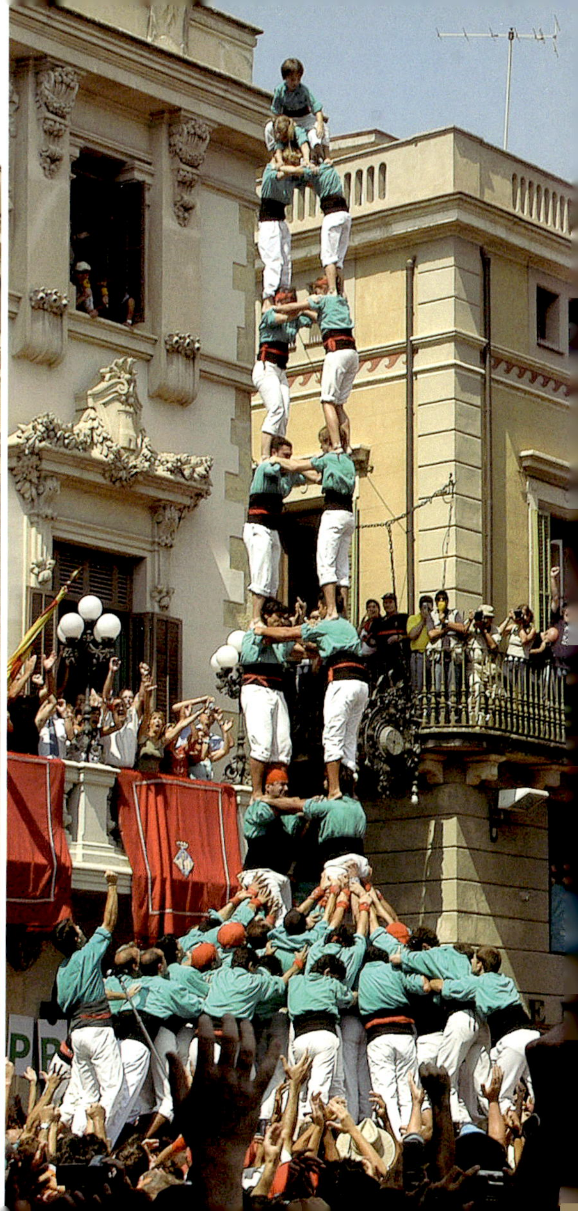

Clear 2 of 8 _ Colla Vella dels Xiquets de Valls      Clear 2 of 8 _ Colla Joves Xiquets de Valls

2 of 9 with *folre* and *manilles* _ Colla Vella dels Xiquets de Valls   2 of 9 with *folre* and *manilles* _ Minyons de Terrassa

2 of 9 with *folre* and *manilles* _ Colla Joves Xiquets de Valls

2 of 9 with *folre* and *manilles* _ Capgrossos de Mataró

**5.** All the *castells*

2 of 8 with *folre*
Castellers de Sants

2 of 8 with *folre*
Colla Jove Xiquets de Tarragona

2 of 8 with *folre*
Castellers de Barcelona

## 5. All the castells

2 of 8 with *folre*
Castellers de Lleida

2 of 8 with *folre*
Castellers de Terrassa

2 of 8 with *folre*
Nens del Vendrell

**5.** All the *castells*

2 of 8 with *folre*
Xiquets de Tarragona

2 of 8 with *folre*
Xicots de Vilafranca

2 of 8 with *folre*
Xiquets de Reus

## 5. All the castells

2 of 7
Castellers de la Vila de Gràcia

2 of 7
Sagals d'Osona

2 of 7
Al·lots de Llevant

**5.** All the *castells*

2 of 7
Minyons de l'Arboç

2 of 7
Castellers de Sant Cugat

2 of 6
Castellers de Caldes de Montbui

## 5. All the *castells*

2 of 9 with *folre* and *manilles* _ Minyons de Terrassa

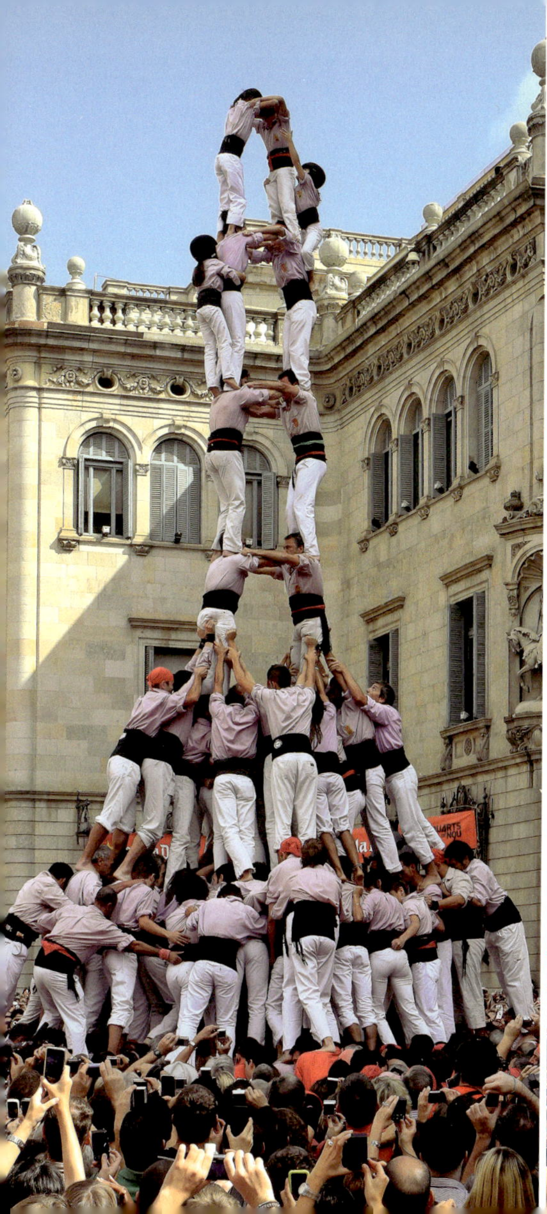

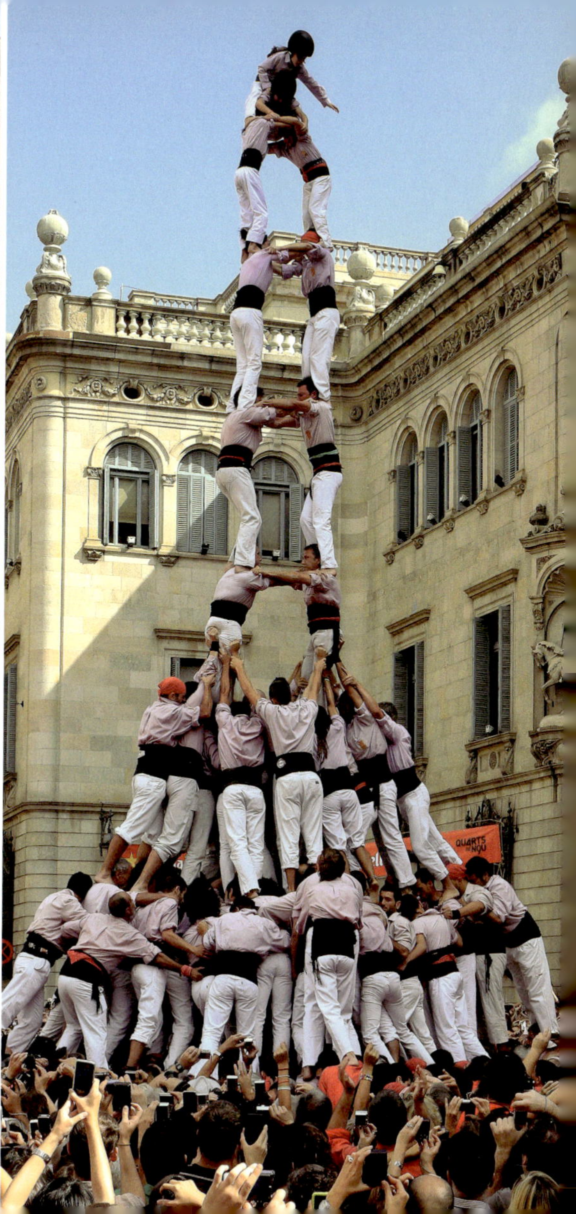

**5.** All the *castells*

# El tres
## The three

Construction of three *castellers* per storey that, strengthened with *folre* and *manilles*, can reach ten storeys, the maximum height ever reached in a *castell*, and which until now has been achieved by three *colles*, the Minyons de Terrassa, the Castellers de Vilafranca and the Colla Vella dels Xiquets de Valls. The first *colla* to build it was that of the Castellers de Vilafranca, and the first to complete it the Minyons de Terrassa. Both featured in a thrilling race to be the first *colla* to *fer l'aleta*, in a magical month of November 1998. The *castell* de *tres* is, for many fans, the most aesthetically perfect. In fact, it had been named simply *el castell*. In the 20th century, the *castell* of nine storeys with *folre* was not built until 1982, by the Colla Vella dels Xiquets de Valls, and was not built and disassembled until 1986, thanks to the Colla Joves Xiquets de Valls. This *castell* has been attempted, unsuccessfully, of nine storeys without *folre*.

3 of 10 with *folre* and *manilles* _ Minyons de Terrassa   ↓3 of 10 with *folre* and *manilles* _ Castellers de Vilafranca

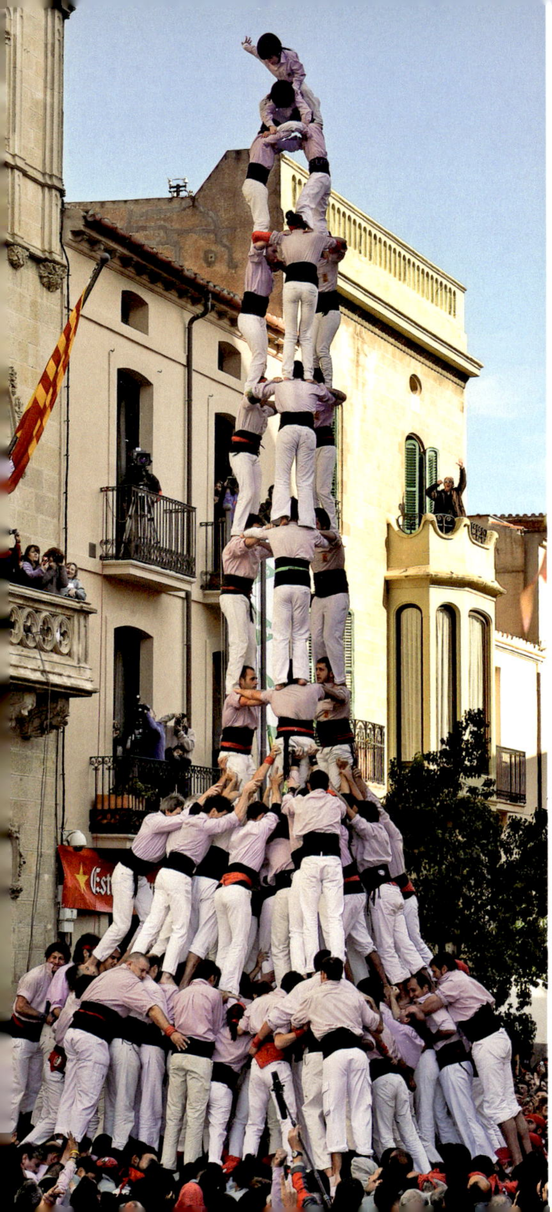

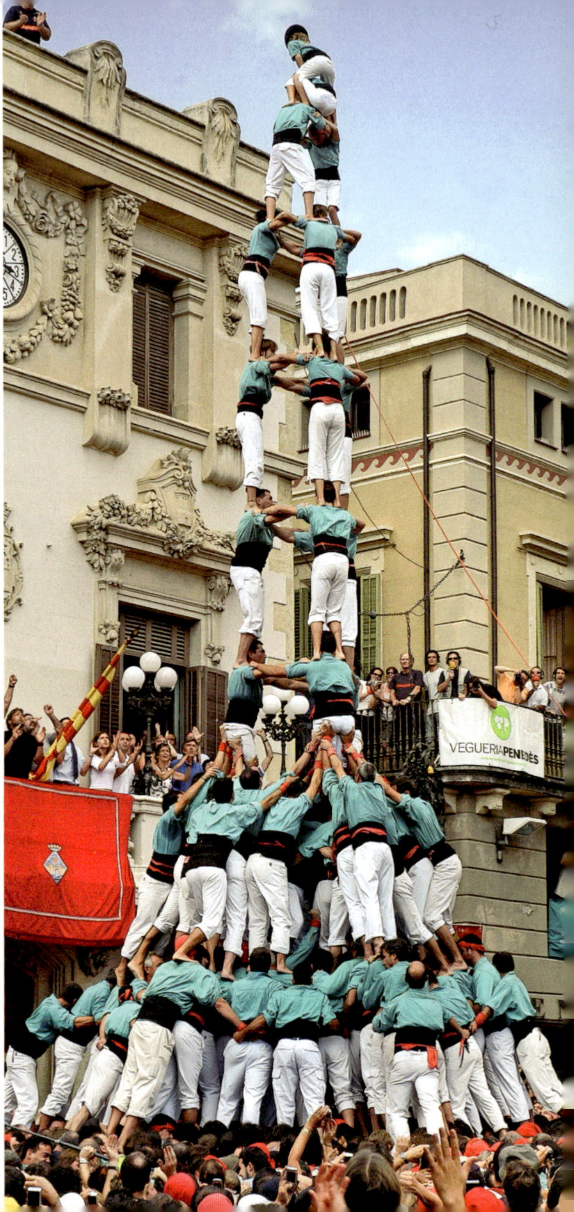
VEGUERIA PENEDÈS

3 of 10 with *folre* and *manilles* _ Colla Vella dels Xiquets de Valls    3 of 9 with *folre* _ Colla Joves Xiquets de Valls

3 of 9 with *folre* _ Capgrossos de Mataró

3 of 9 with *folre* _ Castellers de Sants

3 of 9 with *folre* _ Bordegassos de Vilanova

3 of 9 with *folre* _ Castellers de Barcelona

3 of 9 with *folre* _ Colla Jove Xiquets de Tarragona

3 of 9 with *folre* _ Xiquets de Tarragona

**5.** All the *castells*

3 of 8
Xiquets de Reus

3 of 8
Xicots de Vilafranca

3 of 8
Sagals d'Osona

**5.** All the *castells*

3 of 8
Castellers de Lleida

3 of 8
Castellers de Sabadell

3 of 7
Matossers de Molins de Rei

## 5. All the castells

3 of 7
Salats de Súria

3 of 7
Castellers de Badalona

3 of 7
Torraires de Montblanc

**5.** All the *castells*

3 of 7
Nyerros de la Plana

3 of 6
Castellers de Castelldefels

3 of 6
Colla Jove Xiquets de Vilafranca

**5.** All the *castells*

3 of 10 with *folre* and *manilles* _ Castellers de Vilafranca

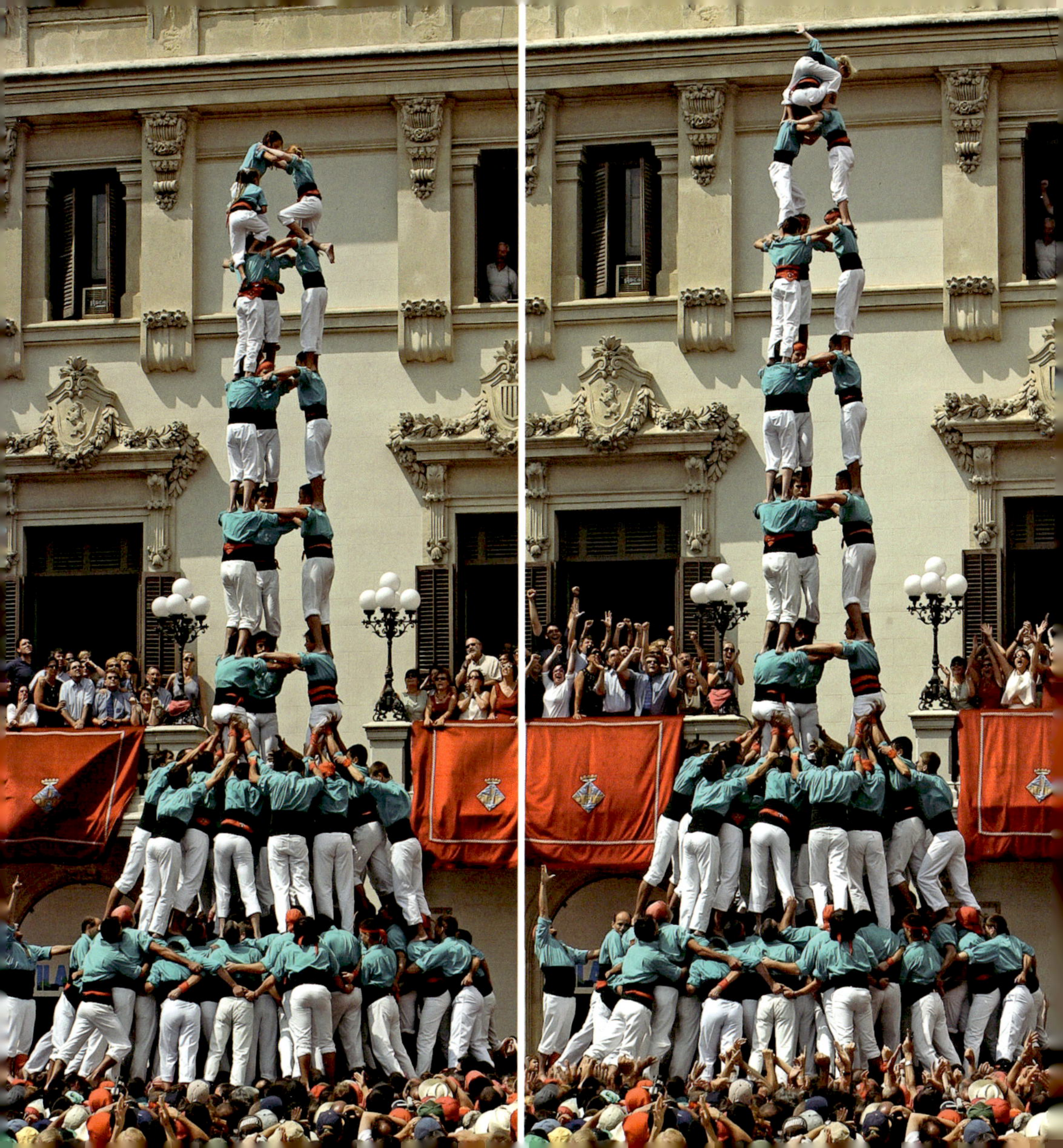

**5.** All the *castells*

# El quatre
## The four

Construction of four *castellers* per storey that can reach a height of nine storeys without any strengthening over the *pinya*. In this version without *folre*, it is called *el castell total*, due to the great technical and physical demand that is made on the *castellers*. It was achieved for the first time by the Colla Vella dels Xiquets de Valls in 1881, and until it was once again achieved, in the 20th century, by the Minyons de Terrassa, who completed it in 1998, it was considered a veritable myth. Usually, in the version of nine storeys, it is built with *folre*. Built in this way, strengthened, it served to recover the *castells* of nine storeys in the 20th century. It was the Colla Vella dels Xiquets de Valls who completed it in the festival of Saint Ursula, in Valls in 1981. In its version of eight storeys, it is the *castell* that the small *colles* currently choose, or they only build *castells* of seven storeys, to take a step forward in their evolution as *castellers*. The four of eight has traditionally been called the *carro gros* (the big carriage), because they say that in the 19th century, there was a very large carriage that was used to move all the *castellers* who formed it from one town to another. The four of ten, strengthened with *folre* and *manilles*, has been unsuccessfully attempted to be built by the Castellers de Vilafranca.

Clear 4 of 9 _ Colla Vella dels Xiquets de Valls ↓ Clear 4 of 9 _ Minyons de Terrassa

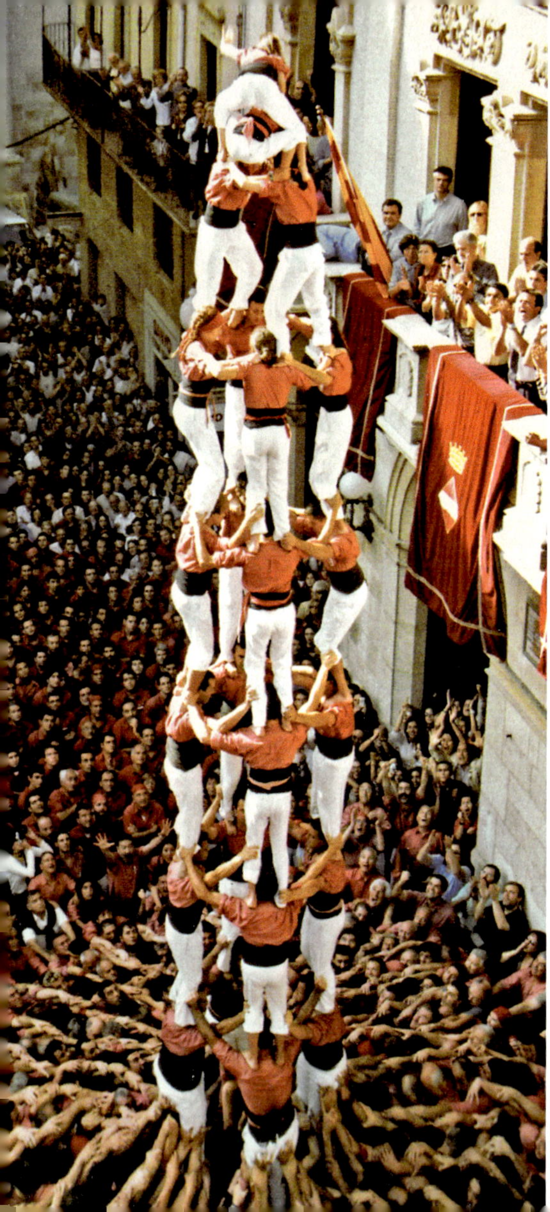

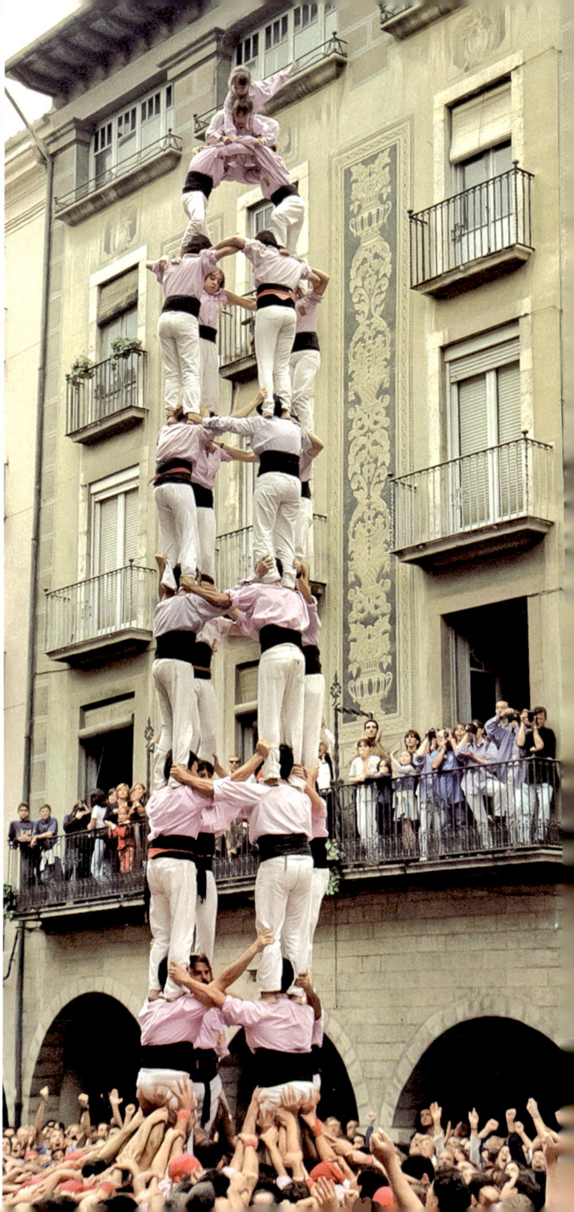

Clear 4 of 9 _ Castellers de Vilafranca

Clear 4 of 9 _ Colla Joves Xiquets de Valls

4 of 9 with *folre* _ Colla Vella dels Xiquets de Valls

4 of 9 with *folre* _ Colla Joves Xiquets de Valls

4 of 9 with *folre* _ Colla Jove Xiquets de Tarragona

4 of 9 with *folre* _ Castellers deSants

4 of 9 with *folre* _ Minyons de Terrassa

4 of 9 with *folre* _ Capgrossos de Mataró

**5.** All the *castells*

4 of 8 _ Xics de Granollers

4 of 8 _ Nens del Vendrell

**5.** All the *castells*

Castellers de Lleida

Xiquets de Reus

4 of 8 _ Castellers de Terrassa

4 of 8 _ Xicots de Vilafranca

4 of 8 _ Castellers de Barcelona

4 of 8 _ Al·lots de Llevant

4 of 8 _ Moixiganguers d'Igualada

4 of 8 _ Colla Jove de Castellers de Sitges

## 5. All the *castells*

4 of 8
Castellers de la Vila de Gràcia

4 of 8
Bordegassos de Vilanova

4 of 8
Sagals d'Osona

**5.** All the *castells*

4 of 7
Castellers de Badalona

4 of 7
Castellers del Riberal

4 of 7
Salats de Súria

## 5. All the *castells*

4 of 7
Castellers de la Sagrada Família

4 of 7
Tirallongues de Manresa

4 of 7
Minyons de l'Arboç

**5.** All the *castells*

4 of 7
Castellers de Cerdanyola

4 of 7
Colla Castellera de Figueres

4 of 6
Castellers de Rubí

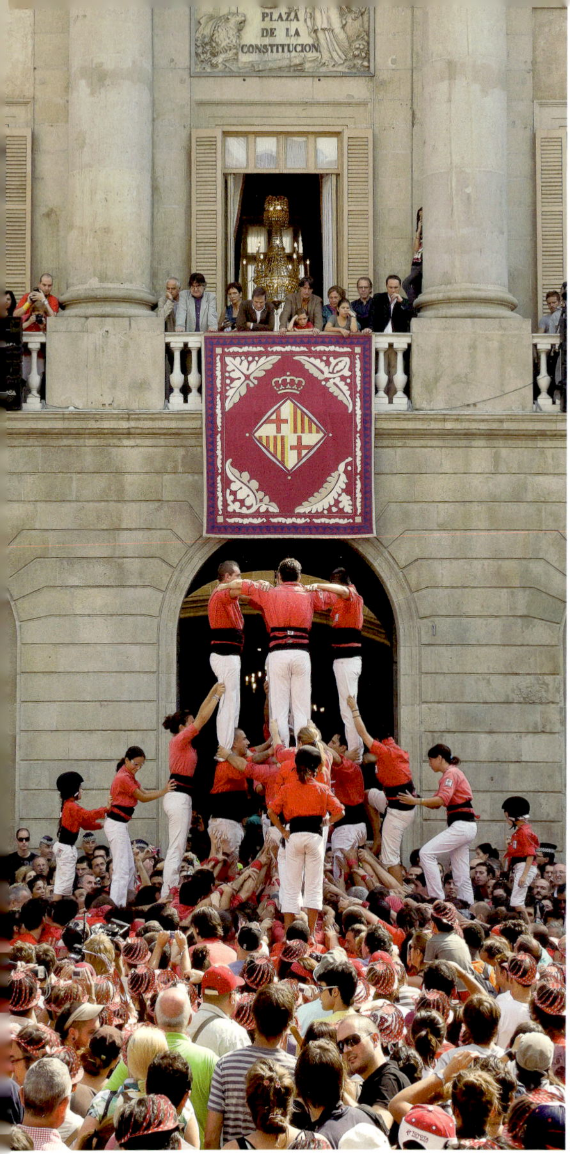

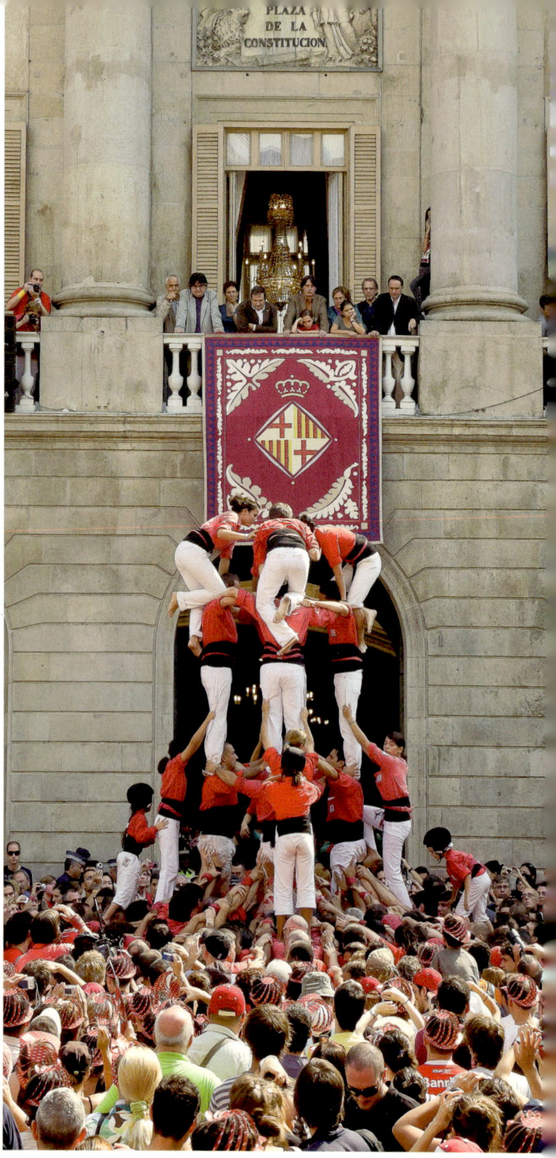


4 of 8 _ Castellers de Barcelona

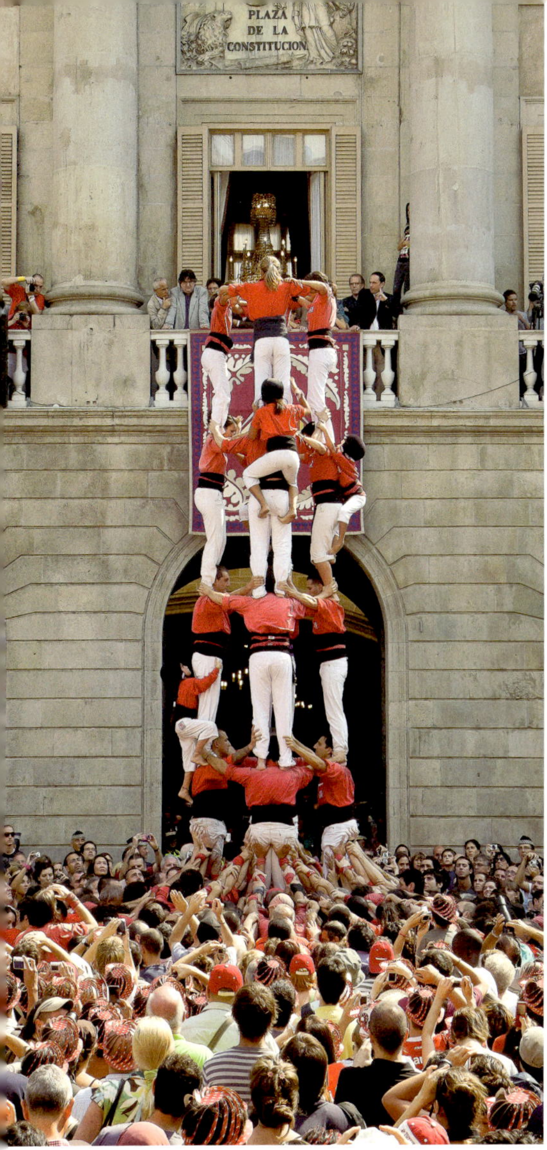
PLAZA
DE LA
CONSTITUCION

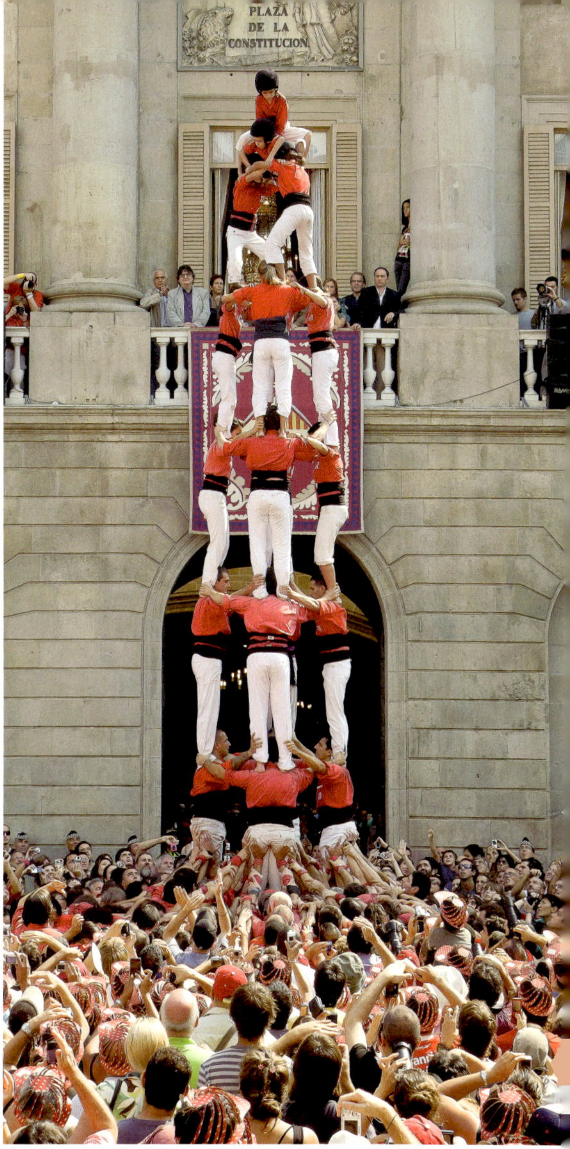
PLAZA
DE LA
CONSTITUCION

## 5. All the *castells*

# El cinc
## The five

Construction of combined structure, made up of a *castell* of three *castellers* per storey, and one, attached to this, of two *castellers* per storey. In this *castell*, the last *casteller* who climbs, the *enxaneta*, must place themselves over both structures, first on that of the three and then on the two, and raise their arm doing the *aleta* both times. The *castell* will not be built until the second *aleta* has been made. The more difficult version, the five of nine with *folre*, was achieved in 19th century by the Colla Vella dels Xiquets de Valls. In the 20th century the first *colla* to build it was the Minyons de Terrassa, in the Barcelona festival of the Mercè in 1995. One year later, the Colla Vella dels Xiquets de Valls completed it. Due to its enormity, the five of eight is called "the cathedral" and, in the version of nine storeys some people refer to it as the "super-cathedral".

5 of 9 with *folre* _ Minyons de Terrassa  ↓ 5 of 9 with *folre* _ Castellers de Vilafranca

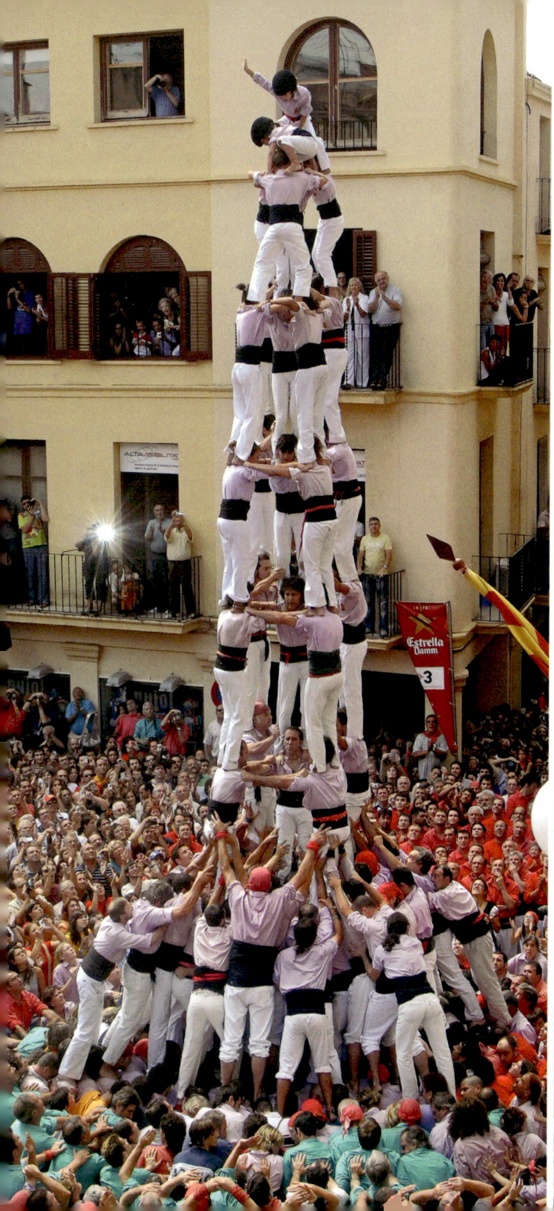
Estrella Damm
3

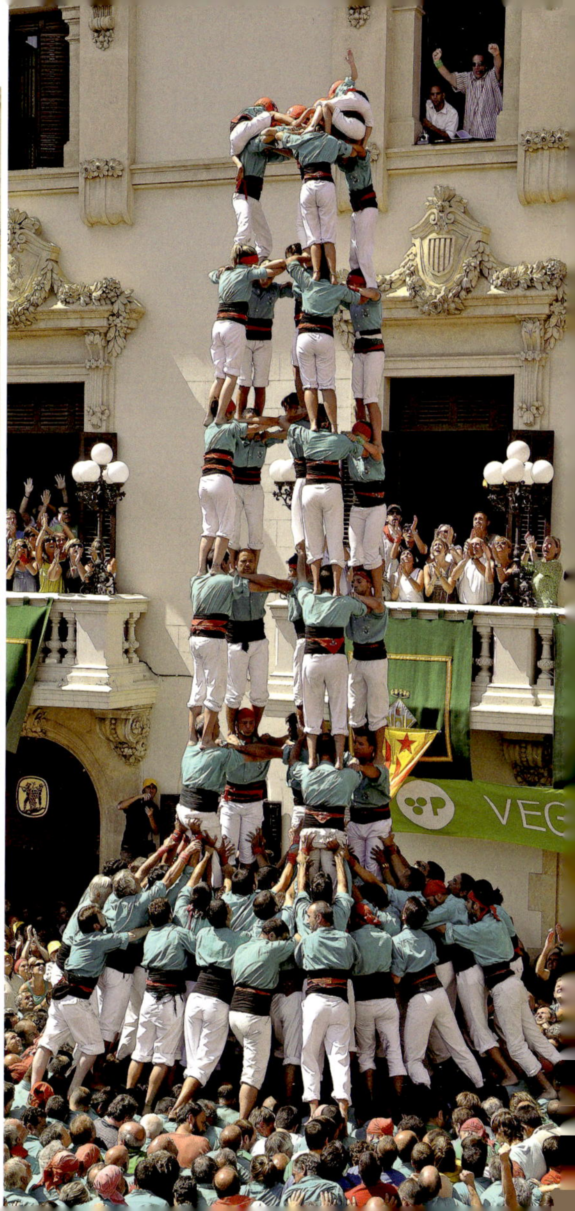
VEG

5 of 9 with *folre* _ Colla Joves Xiquets de Valls

5 of 9 with *folre* _ Colla Vella dels Xiquets de Valls

5 of 8 _ Colla Joves Xiquets de Valls

5 of 8 _ Colla Vella dels Xiquets de Valls

**5.** All the *castells*

5 of 8 _ Castellers de Sants

5 of 8 _ Capgrossos de Mataró

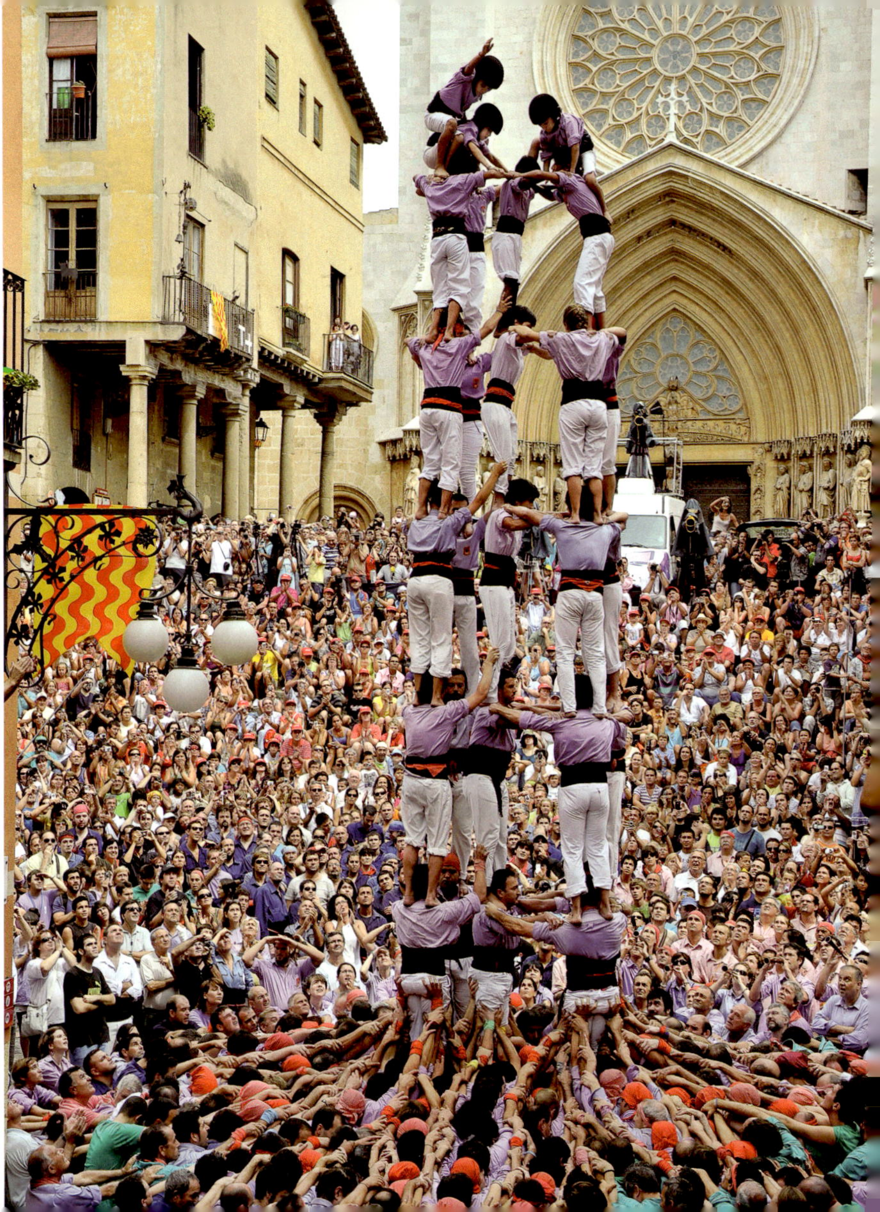

5 of 8 _ Colla Jove Xiquets de Tarragona

## 5. All the *castells*

5 of 8 _ Xiquets de Tarragona

5 of 8 _ Bordegassos de Vilanova

**5.** All the *castells*

5 of 7
Colla Jove de Castellers de Sitges

5 of 7
Nois de la Torre

5 of 7
Castellers de Barcelona

## 5. All the *castells*

5 of 7
Castellers d'Esplugues

5 of 7
Xics de Granollers

5 of 7
Castellers del Poble Sec

**5.** All the *castells*

5 of 7
Castellers de Cornellà

5 of 7
Castellers de la Vila de Gràcia

5 of 7
Castellers d'Esparreguera

## 5. All the *castells*

Margeners de Guissona

**5.** All the *castells*

5 of 7
Xicots de Vilafranca

5 of 7
Marrecs de Salt

5 of 7
Minyons de l'Arboç

**5.** All the *castells*

# El quatre amb l'agulla o el pilar al mig

## The four with point, or pillar, in the middle

Compound construction made up of a *castell* of four *castellers* per storey, and a pillar that is situated in the centre of the four. The pillar in the middle is built at the same time as the *castell* and the *aixecador* (or sometimes the *enxaneta*) crowns it, and goes from there to the pillar. It is one of the most spectacular *castells* due to its complexity in construction. When the *castellers* of the four climb down from the *castell*, the pillar appears alone over the *pinya* and the structure is considered built. When the *castellers* of the pillar have been able to descend, it is considered complete. In its most difficult version, made up of four of nine with *folre* and a pillar of seven inside, it was not built until 1995. The Castellers de Vilafranca achieved it and this same *colla*, which over time has become the real specialist in this construction, completed it a year later. As we mentioned, this *castell* is very complex, and the *colles* must dominate both a different technique when constructing the *pinya* and that of the large pillars.

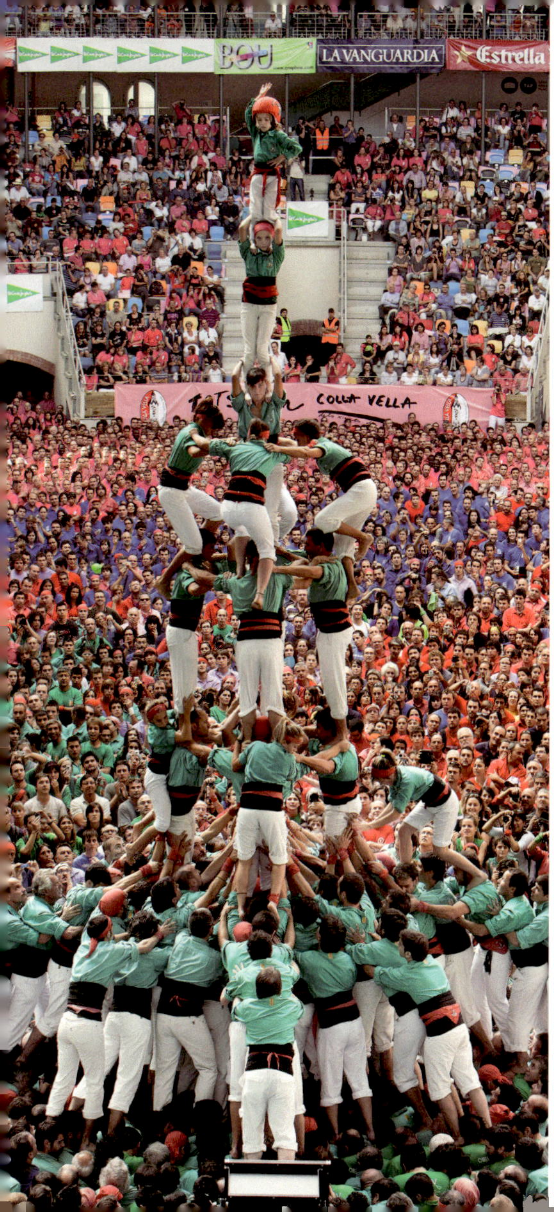
BOU
LA VANGUARDIA
Estrella
COLLA VELLA

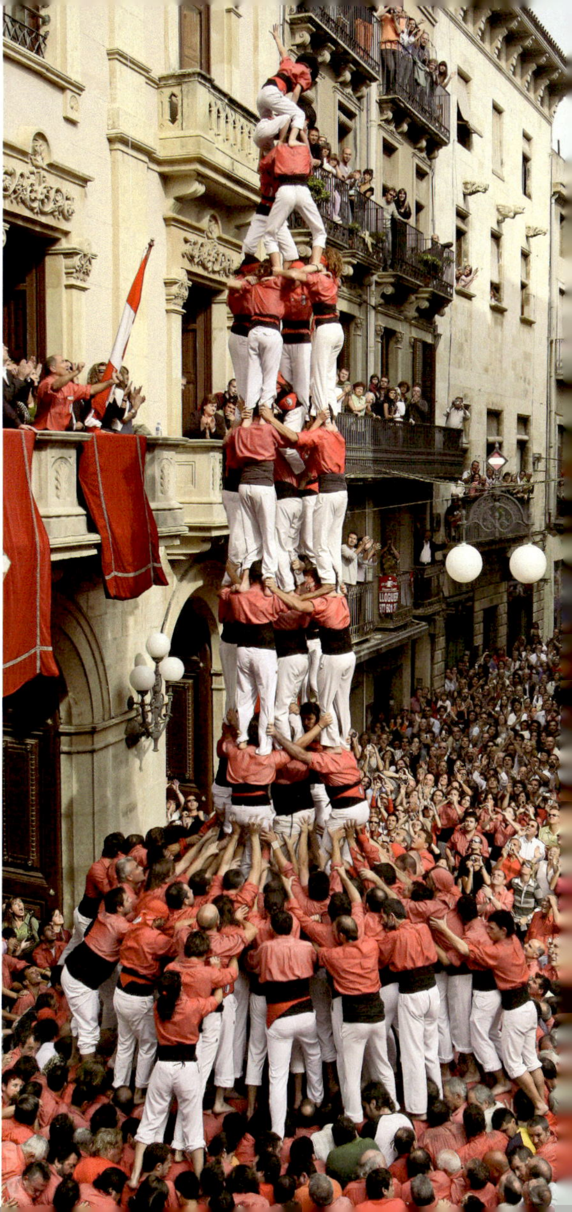

**5.** All the *castells*

4 of 8 with point _ Castellers de Barcelona

4 of 8 with point _ Xiquets de Tarragona

4 of 9 with *folre* and *point* _ Minyons de Terrassa

**5.** All the *castells*

4 of 7 with point _ Castellers de Sants

4 of 7 with point _ Castellers de Sant Pere i Sant Pau

**5.** All the *castells*

4 of 7 with point _ Xiquets del Serrallo

4 of 7 with point _ Colla Jove de Castellers de Sitges

## 5. All the castells

4 of 7 with point
Castellers d'Altafulla

4 of 7 with point
Castellers del Poble Sec

4 of 7 with point
Castellers de la Sagrada Família

## 5. All the castells

4 of 7 with point
Castellers de la Vila de Gràcia

4 of 7 with point
Castellers de Cerdanyola

4 of 6 with point
Nois de la Torre

4 of 9 with *folre* and point _ Castellers de Vilafranca

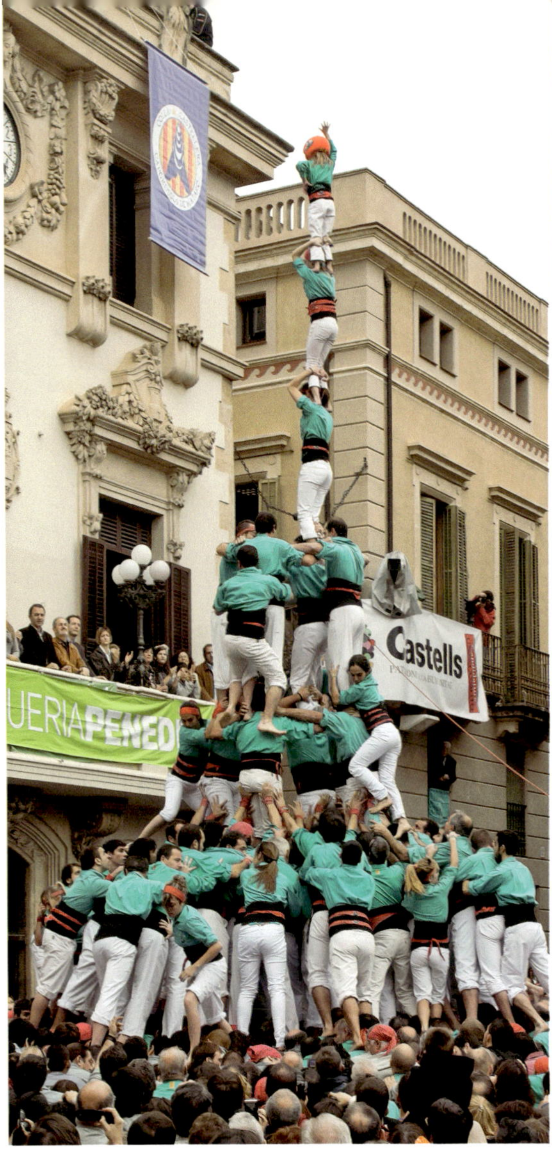
GUERIAPENED
Castells

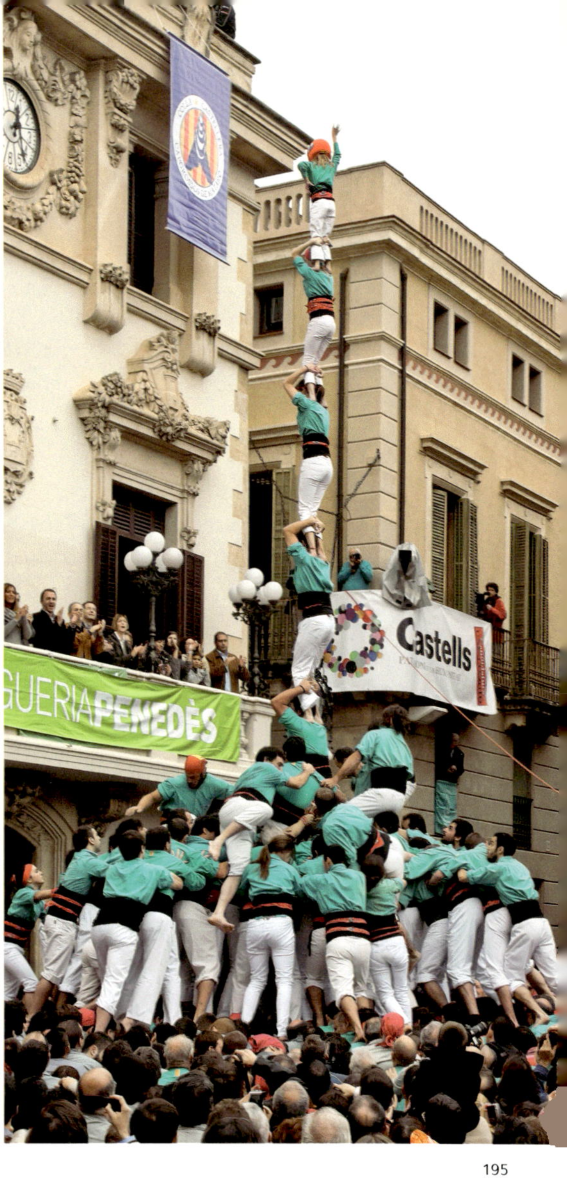
GUERIAPENEDÈS
Castells

**5.** All the *castells*

# El tres amb l'agulla o el pilar al mig

## The three with point, or pillar, in the middle

Compound construction made up of a *castell* of three *castellers* per storey, and a pillar placed in the middle of the three. It is therefore basically a construction very similar to the four with pillar in the middle. In its version of eight and nine storeys, with a pillar of six and seven in the middle respectively, it is one of the latest innovations in the world of *castells*. In fact, the three of nine with *folre* and point in the middle was built for the first time ever in November 2008, in the city of Terrassa and was achieved by the local *colla*, the Minyons de Terrassa. However, less than a year later, In August 2009, the Castellers de Vilafranca were the first to complete it. The three with point in the middle is a *castell* with some detractors, who consider it a poor copy of its predecessor, the four with point in the middle. In any case, it is unarguable that we are before a *castell* that, in its version of nine storeys, is extremely difficult and spectacular.

3 of 9 with *folre* and point _ Minyons de Terrassa ↓ 3 of 9 with *folre* and point _ Castellers de Vilafranca

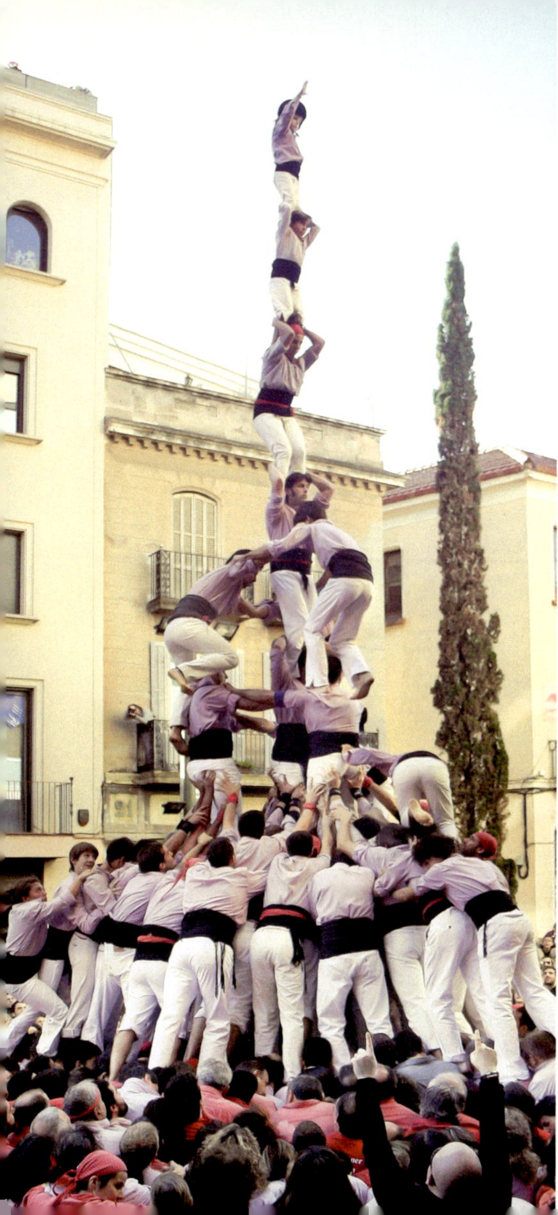

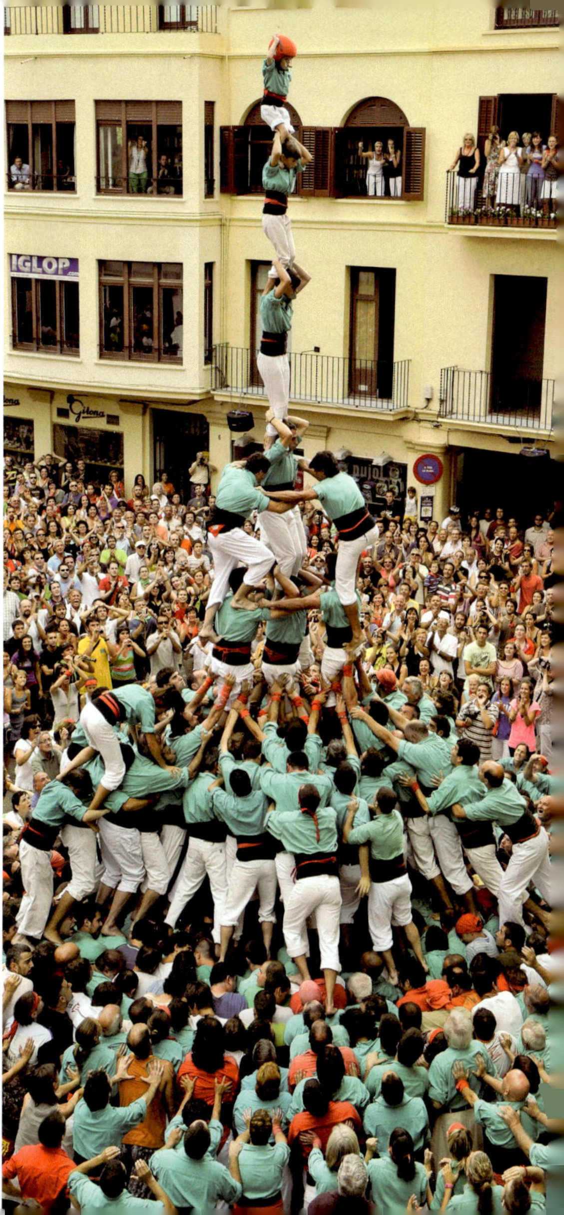
IGLOP
Gilona

## 5. All the *castells*

3 of 8 with point _ Castellers de Barcelona

3 of 7 with point _ Castellers del Poble Sec

**5.** All the *castells*

3 of 7 with point _ Castellers de Sant Pere i Sant Pau

3 of 6 with point _ Colla Castellera Jove de Barcelona

3 of 8 with the pillar in the middle _ Colla Joves Xiquets de Valls

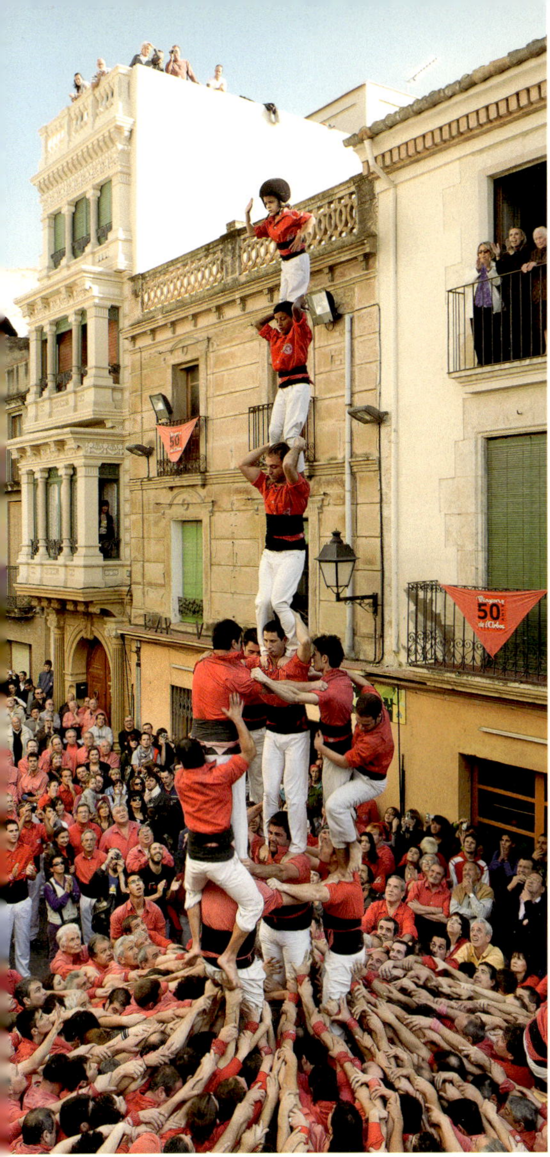

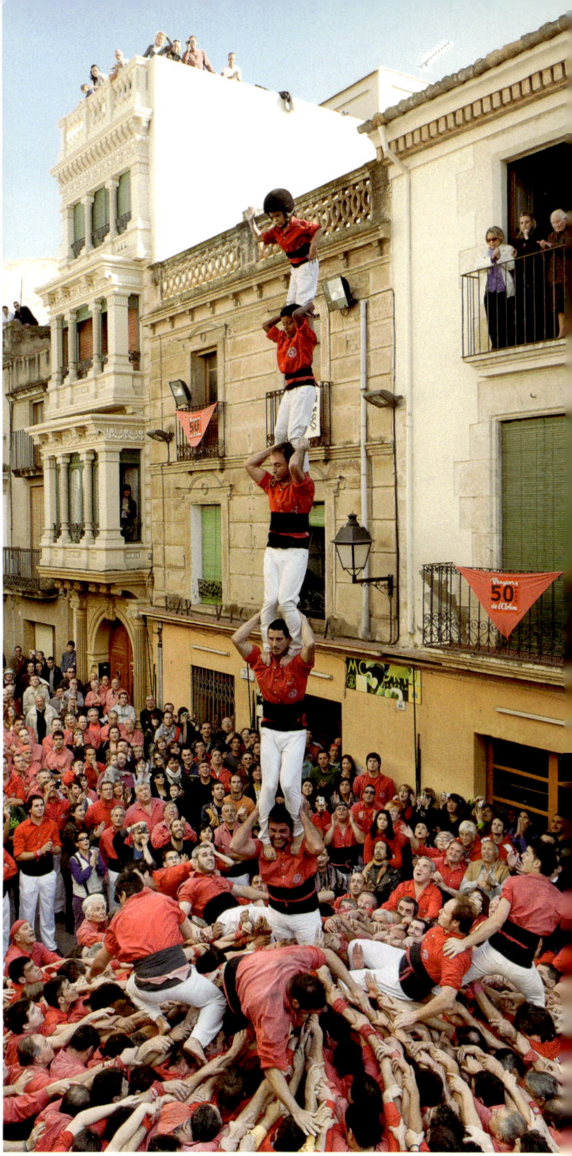

**5.** All the *castells*

# El tres aixecat per sota, o per baix

## The three raised from below

Construction of three *castellers* per storey that, in its most difficult version, reaches eight storeys in height. It is built in reverse to the great majority of *castells*, that is, not climbing one *casteller* over the other, but rather raising the weight, in a measured way, of the *castellers* of the various storeys of the *castell* and placing them beneath a new storey. Thus, the first *castellers* that appear above the *pinya* are the smallest, who slowly rise up as the storeys below are constructed. Having reached its maximum height, and the *enxaneta* has done the *aleta*, the *castellers* descend using the regular technique as in the majority of *castells*. In its version of seven storeys, it is a fairly common *castell*, but the version of eight is quite unusual and of the utmost difficulty. It had already been completed in the 19th century, but in the 20th century very few *colles* attempted it. Apart from the difficulty of slowly raising the weight of a construction made up of so many people with losing their balance and making it fall, we should take into account the danger of a fall, since, in this sense, while a *castell* is raised, the *pinya* is not compact because the *castellers* that it lifts need a space to place themselves and make the effort comfortably. This situation, therefore, decreases the effectiveness of the *pinya* as an absorbing element of falls. The Colla Vella dels Xiquets de Valls was the first to build and disassemble the three of eight raised from below in the 20th century. It was in 1999 in the town of Vila-rodona.

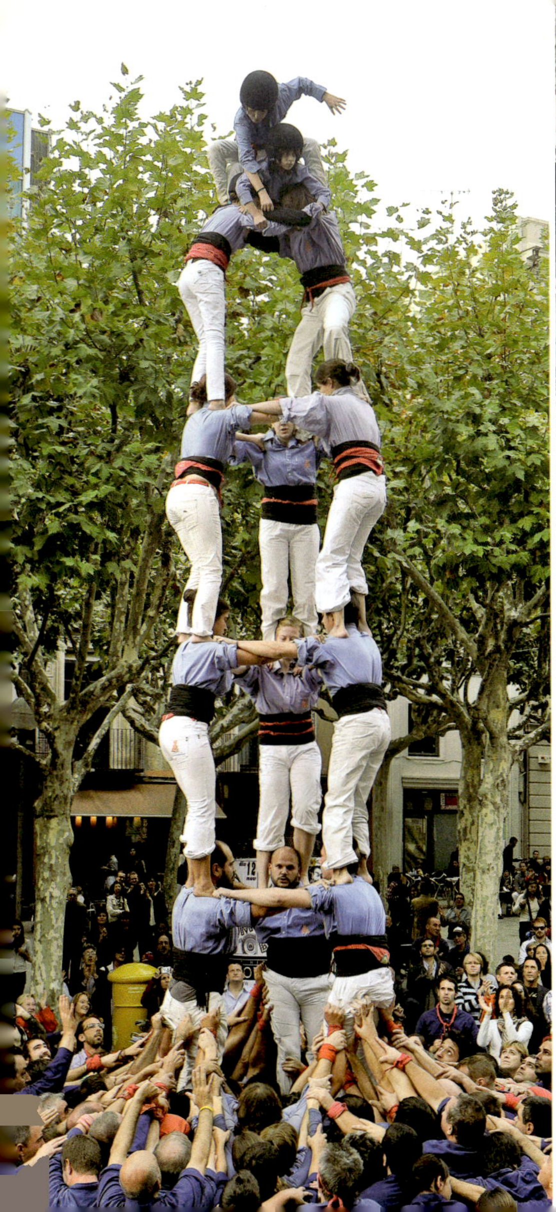

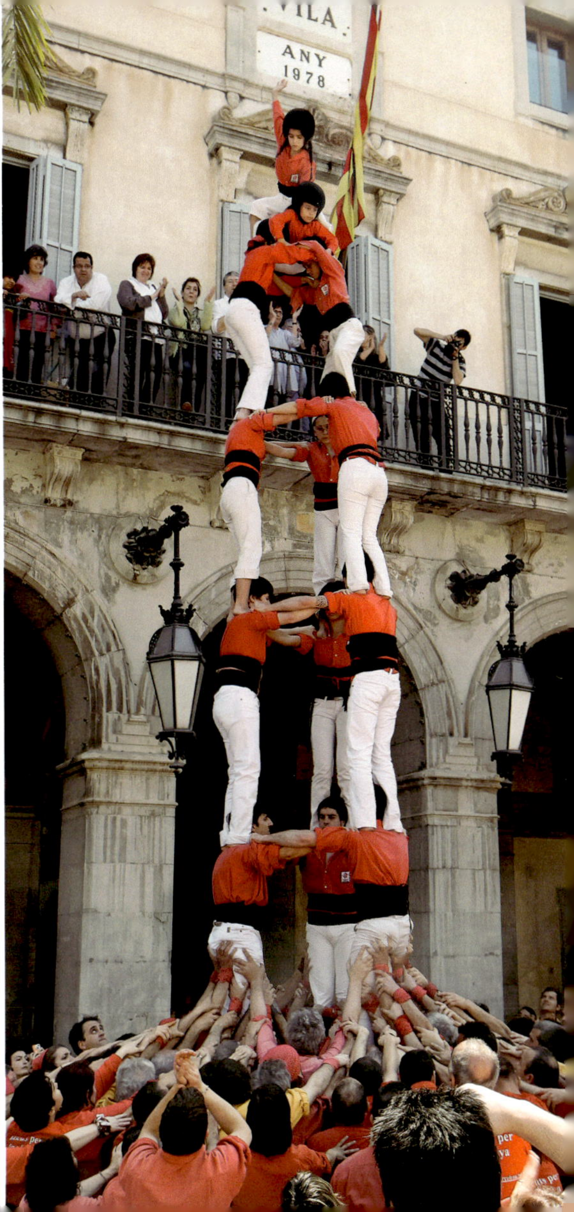
VILA
ANY
1978

3 of 8 raised from below _ Colla Vella dels Xiquets de Valls
Building the storeys gently and regularly is vital to achieve this type of *castell*, extraordinarily difficult.
The *enxaneta* waits behind the *dosos* while the *castell* rises. After, they take their place over the *aixecador*
and salute

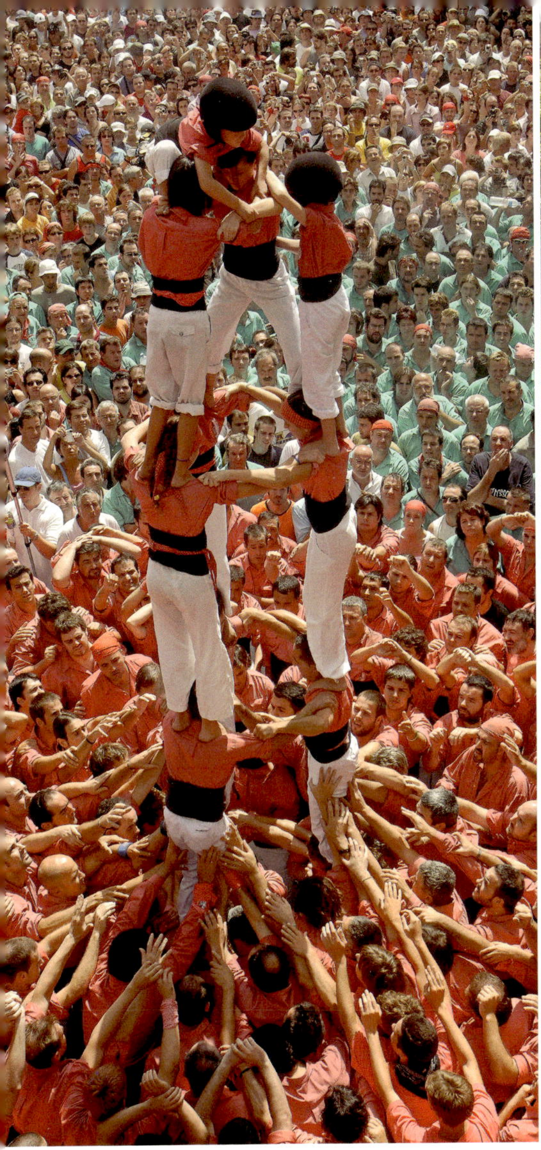

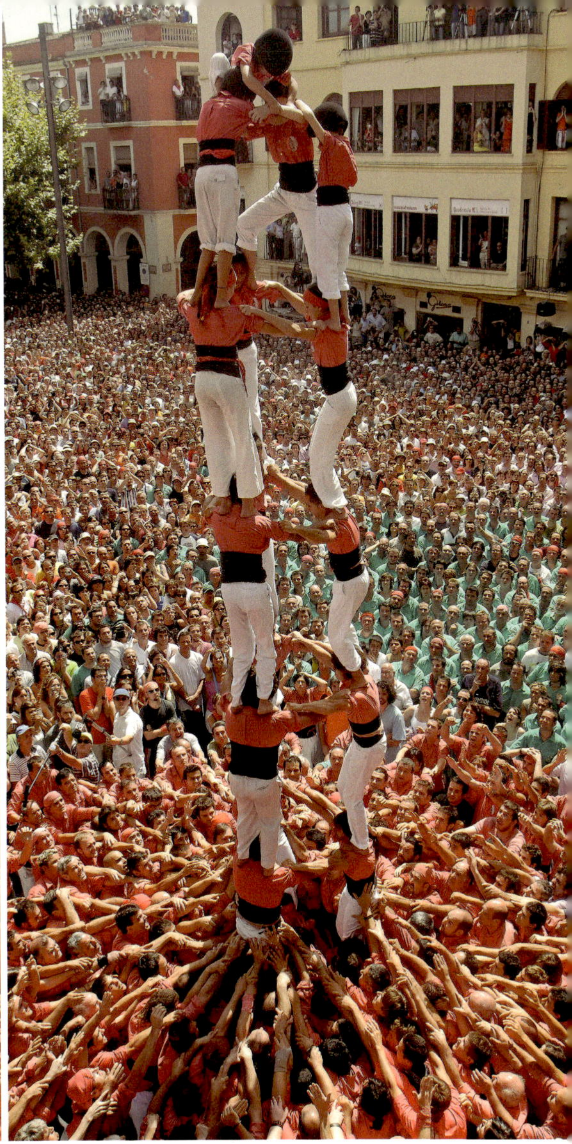

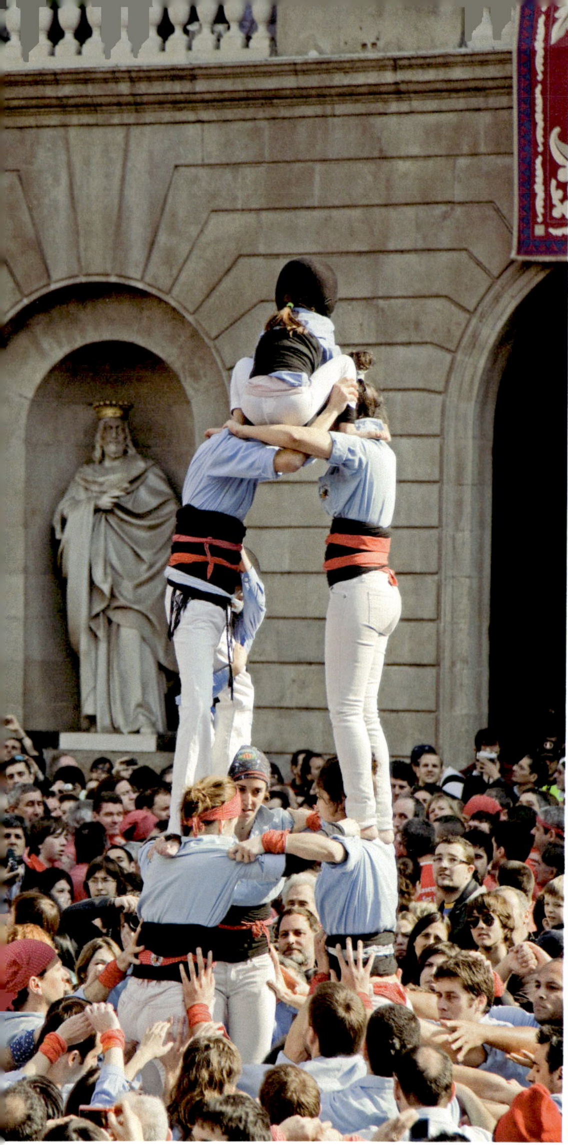
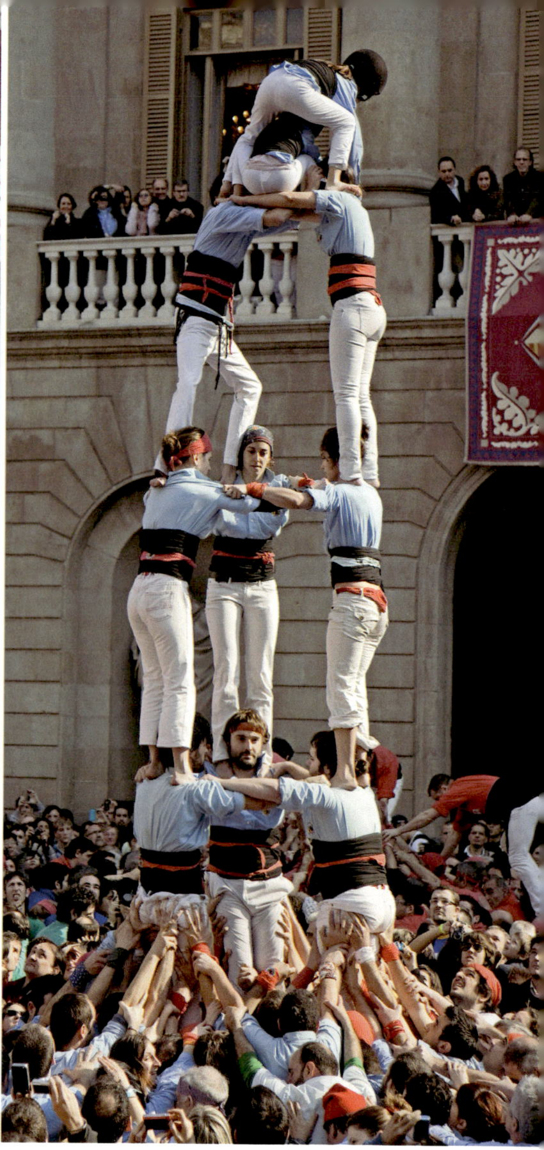

3 of 6 raised from below _ Castellers del Poble Sec

2 of 7 raised from below _ Castellers de Sants

## 5. All the *castells*

# The *castells* also fall

A priori, the *castells* are perfect structures. Nevertheless, the balance of forces that intervene and the demand for concentration by the *castellers* can make them vulnerable. This is why they also fall apart and collapse. If they fall before the *enxaneta* has raised their arm doing the *aleta* it is said that that it has been only an "attempt", and has no value. If they fall after doing the *aleta* it is said that it has only been built, and its value is less than those that have not fallen in the disassembly and are completed. We should point out that in the 19th century, unlike today, the *castells* only had any value if they were completed. In general, it is considered that a *castell* has been completed or disassembled when it or the *castellers* of the storey that climbing, have marked the beginning of the construction, climb down by themselves. As we have said, it is easy to know when a *castell* begins: at the same time as the music starts. Avoiding falls is the main objective, not always achieved, of the *colles*. That is why, on occasions, the person leading the *castell* from the ground, the *cap de colla*, commands the *castellers* of the *tronc* who disassemble a *castell* that it is not secure enough before the *aleta* is done. In this case, it will be a "disassembled attempt". Despite the spectacular nature of the falls, the *castellers* do not generally get hurt, but it is also the case that, like any accident in a sport or physical activity, it may cause injuries.

Fall of a pillar. Colla Jove Xiquets de Tarragona

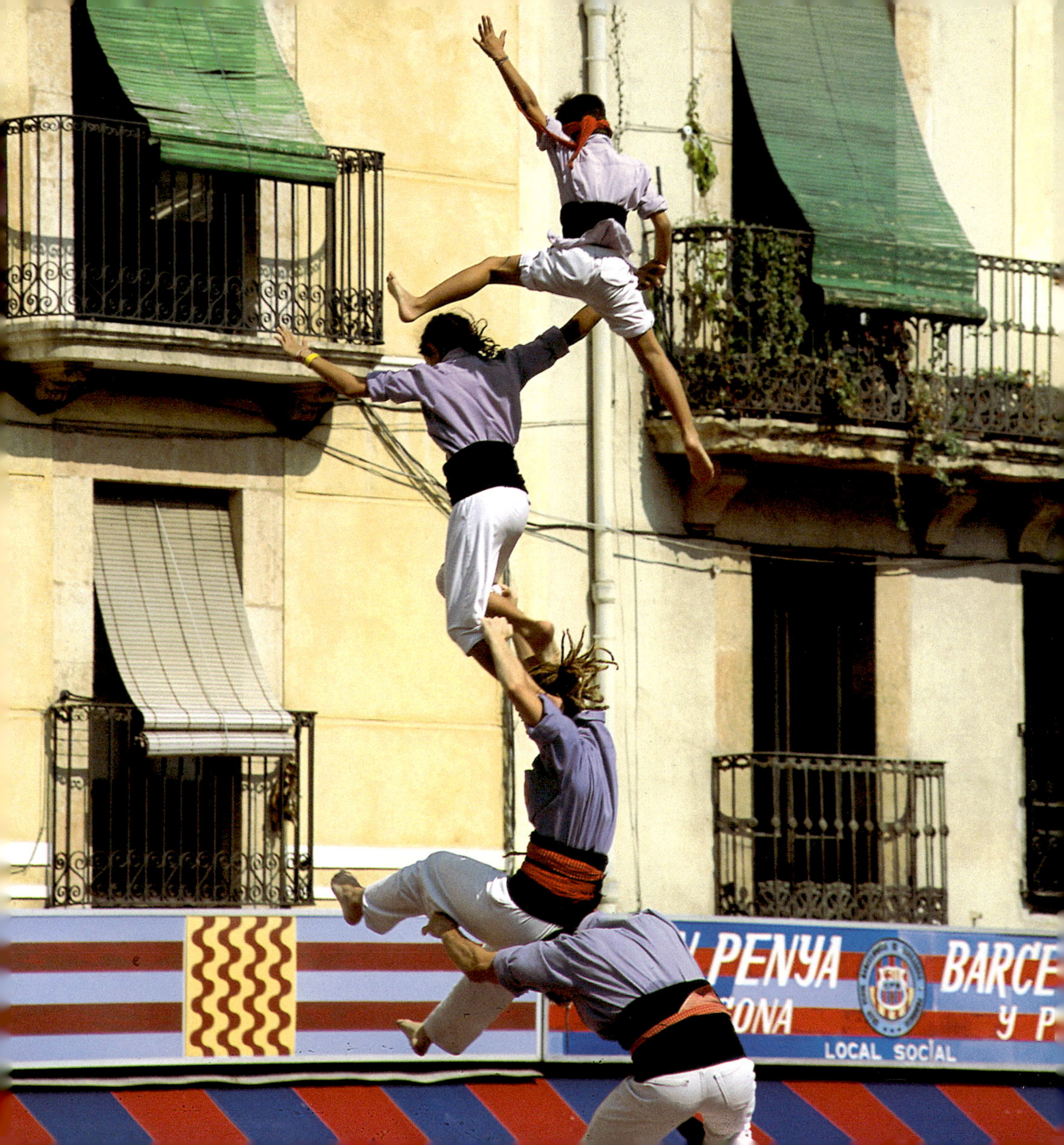
PENYA
BARCE
ONA
Y P
LOCAL SOCIAL

Fall of a 4 of 8. Bordegassos de Vilanova

Fall of a Tower of 7. Xicots de Vilafranca

TARRAGONA
Patrimoni Mundial
TARRAGONA
Patrimoni Mundial

# 6. The *Diades*

## The rules

Curiously, the world of *castells*, with more than two hundred years of existence, dos not have any written rules, common and accepted by all the *colles*, and which controls their activity. Nevertheless, this does not mean that it is an anarchic activity. There are a set of minimum standards, some conventions, the result of tradition and evolution, which are complied with in nearly all the *diades*.

In a standard *diada* that complies with the more basic conventions, we could witness the following steps: before starting the performance, the *caps de colla* take part in a draw to establish, on the one hand, which position each *colla* will occupy in the square and, on the other hand, the order of turns. Just minutes before the event begins, the *colles* enter the square with a pillar of four that they walk to the spot they will occupy. Once all the *colles* have entered, the event starts properly.

A *diada* is undertaken based on this description: "Three rounds and pillar", in other words, at a conventional event, each *colla* usually makes three *castells*, and ends with a pillar. Each part of a performance is called *ronda* (round), and in each round a *colla* makes a *castell*. When, for example, the three *colles* taking part in a *diada* have completed their first *castell*, or the possibility of making it, the first round ends. From here on, however, there may be several variations, depending on which *colla*, *diada* or city is involved. Therefore, there are *diades* with one or two rounds of improvement in the last of the three conventional rounds, where the *colles* that have not achieved a *castell* in one of the rounds, or who want to try a more complex one, have the right to make another construction. It is also common for a *colla* that has not achieved the *castell* announced in a round, to try again, or repeat, within the same round but immediately, or after the performance of the following *colla* or *colles* in the established order.

## 6. The *diades*

To know which *colla* has given the best performance, the importance of the *castells* made in the three rounds and the round of pillars are always counted.

## The value of the *castells*

There are different variables to determine the difficulty and, as a consequence, the value of the *castells*. One, obviously, is the height. For example, a three of eight is more difficult than a three of seven, and is valued more. However, between a three of eight and a five of eight, different *castells* but of the same height, the five of eight has more value because it is more complex. The valuation of the *castells* is partly the result of tradition, of the difficulty that the *colles* experience to make it, or of conventionalisms, and has registered small variations over the years. In general, nevertheless, the *colles*, as well as the fans and the specialised press, value the *castells* that are built in the *diades* according to an agreed points table which is applied at the Castells de Tarragona Competition, which can be consulted, as mentioned, at the website www.concursdecastells.cat.

As we explained to you when speaking of the most important *diada* in the *casteller* calendar, that of the Castells Competition of Tarragona, it is here where the rules reach their maximum forcefulness. The point given for a *castell* may involve the chronometer, but especially the evaluation of the technical refinement in its execution. For example, if an *enxaneta* or *aixecador* does not place their feet correctly, or climbs or descends on the wrong side, they will be penalised, unlike what happens in a conventional *diada*.

In fact, some media outlets produce a classification of the *colles* during the season, a league table, according to the value of the *castells* they have made. It is a journalistic resource that enables the press to explain more didactically the progress of the season, and valuate with more objective criteria the quality at that moment of the *colles*.

It is also true that some people think that the *castells* cannot be given points because their difficulty is not standard, but depends on the particularities of each *colla*.

**6.** The *diades*

Capgrossos de Mataró, celebrating the success of a *castle*

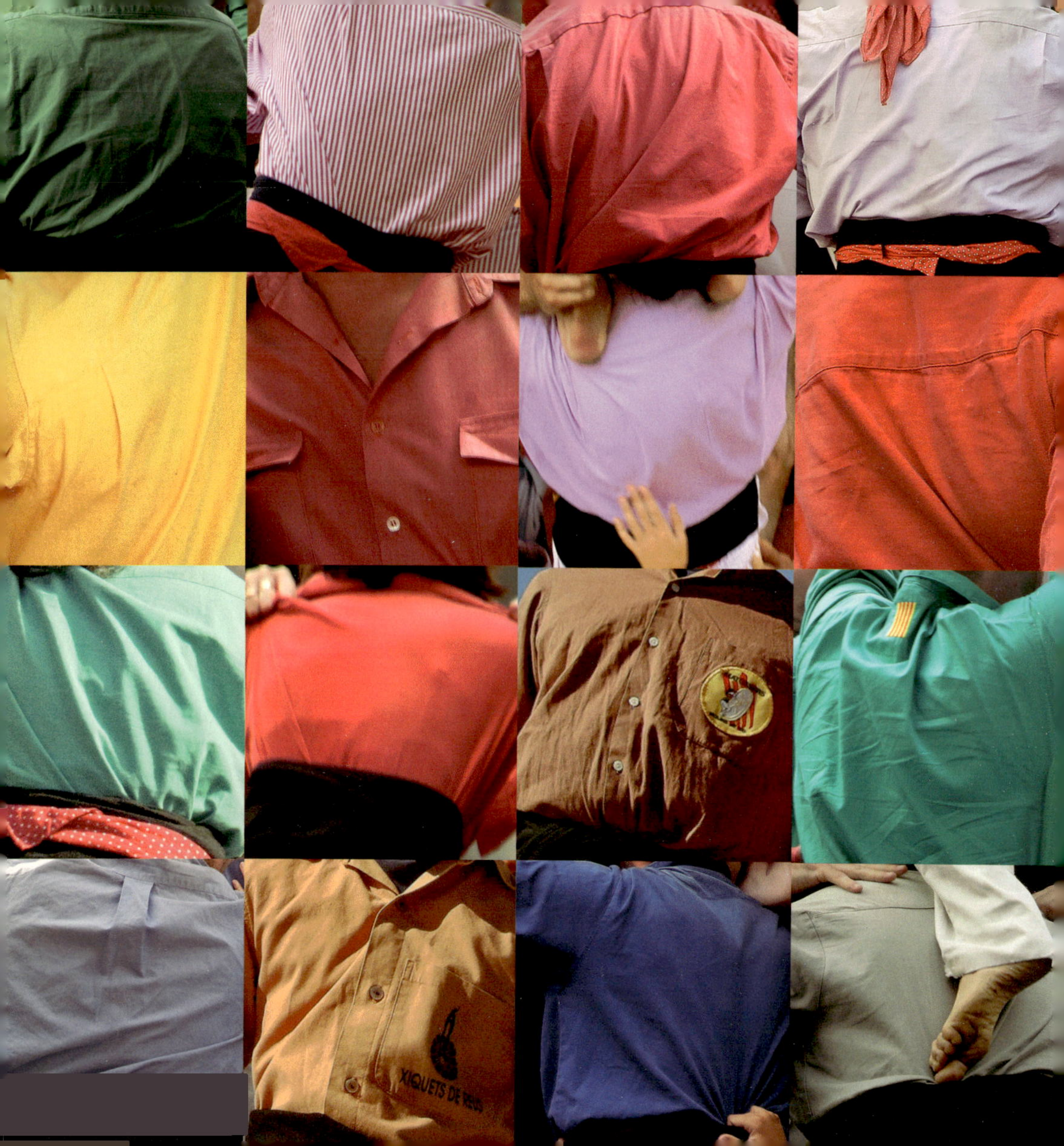
XIQUETS DE REUS

# 7. The *colles*

Today's *colles* have nothing in common with the early ones of the 19th century. The modern *colles* are perfectly organised like, for example, any sports club or association. They have a headquarters and a rehearsal space, a set of statutes, accounts, logistics section, computer equipment... They are a small world, like a small company that has to be made to work every day. In contrast, until well into the 20th century, the *colles* were very precariously organised and depended on the willingness of people and on the leadership exercised by its *cap de colla*. Also, very often, its *castellers* made *castells* in order to get a bonus on top of their wages, unlike today, where nobody gets paid to do this activity.

There are some sixty *colles* spread around Catalonia and the Balearic Islands. Each *colla* is distinguished by a different colour shirt with, generally, a badge sewn onto the shirt pocket. In the cities of Tarragona, Valls, Vilafranca, Terrassa and Barcelona there are more than one, but it is more common that each town has just one *colla* that represents it. Practically all the *colles* have a website, where the followers, fans and *castellers* can keep up to date with events. Apart from the cities mentioned, there are also *colles* of *castellers* in Reus, Vilanova i la Geltrú, Mataró, Salt, Lleida, Vic, Granollers, Palma de Mallorca, Manacor, Torredembarra, Altafulla, L'Arboç, Olot, Cornellà, Sabadell, Igualada,

## 7. The *colles*

Figueres, Sitges, El Vendrell, Bao (Roussillon, France) and Manresa, among others. As we can see, all the *colles* mentioned are in the territory of the old Catalan-Aragonese crown. Nevertheless, diverse *colles* have been formed, in a more nominal way, in Catalan cultural centres abroad, such as Mexico and Argentina. Today there are also healthy *colles castelleres* in Chile and China, thanks to the international promotional work undertaken by *colles* such as the Castellers de Vilafranca and the Colla Vella dels Xiquets de Valls.

3 of 8 _ Colla Vella dels Xiquets de Valls. Shanghai

Tower of 8 _ Castellers de Vilafranca. Santiago de Chile          3 of 7 _ Castellers de lo Prado. Chile

**7.** The *colles*

## The rehearsals

They have always been part and parcel of the *castells*, and still are in the 21st century. Today, the *colles* have systemised the rehearsals or training of the *castells*, which they do several times during the week, with specific trials. Before attempting a *castell* in public, the *colles* rehearse it in their centre in parts, or almost complete. Generally, the rehearsals are open to fans. So if you are interested in discovering in depth the workings of a *colla*, or the technical specifics of the *castells* that in a *diada* you might not notice, you can turn up at a rehearsal centre, especially on Fridays, which is when they usually do the final trials before the weekend performances.

## The centres

Many *colles* currently have a headquarters or centre that is rented or owned by them, and which basically fulfils the functions of rehearsal centre and meeting point of the *castellers*. It can also be used as cafeteria, restaurant, meeting rooms, audiovisual space… Basically, the headquarters is the nerve centre of the *colles*, because it enables them to unite its *castellers* and strengthen its identity. The *colles* often make their centres available to other associations, which open them up even more to the rest of the community.

## The budget of the *colla*

The budget of a *colla* mainly varies according to its size, the cost of maintaining its centre, the operational costs, functioning costs, transport and the leisure activities it organises for its members. The biggest *colles* may close their financial year with movements of more than one hundred and fifty thousand euro. Basically, the income of the *colles* comes from the money that the organisers of the *diades* pay them, the sponsorship agreements they may make with private entities, the occasional use of their centre and subsidies from the public administration for being considered cultural, non-profit bodies. In recent times, the *colles* have introduced fund-raising systems, establishing the figure of the protective member, who pays an annual subscription that helps fund the operating costs. Therefore you can be a *casteller* and protec-

Minyons de l'Arboç

# 7. The *colles*

tive member, or simply a fan of a *colla* and want to collaborate in a different way to that of making *castells*.

## The cost of a performance

There is no standard price. The *colles* get paid according to their potential, the size of their *castells*, the budget of the organisers of the *diades* or the costs that a performance represents for them. Basically, however, the price set must cover, as a minimum, the transport costs of the *castellers*. A *colla* may perform for less than five hundred euros and for more than six thousand. Sometimes, the organisers place a price on a *castell*, in other words, they inform the participating *colles* that if they make a specific *castell*, they will receive a bonus. Sometimes it is also the *colles* that put a price on their *castells*, and inform the organisers that if they want to see one or more of a higher category, they will have to pay extra. There are also *diades* where the *colles* do not get paid, and act in exchange, in other words a *colla* performs alongside another without being paid in exchange for the other performing another day by their side, also without payment.

## Managementof the *casteller* world

Currently the *colles* have formed a body that represents them and safeguards some of their interests, although they have not given up the idea of conserving their independence in their own management and activity. This body is the Coordinating Committee of Colles Castelleres of Catalonia. Among other functions, the Coordinating Committee acts as spokesperson and representative of the *casteller* world and manages subsidies as well as consolidating safety measures. Consulting its website, www.cccc.cat, gives you online access to all the existing *colles*, all the events scheduled on the *casteller* calendar, and consultations about the latest information regarding the Casteller Museum, based in the city of Valls, a setting that provides a broad and historical view of the *castells*.

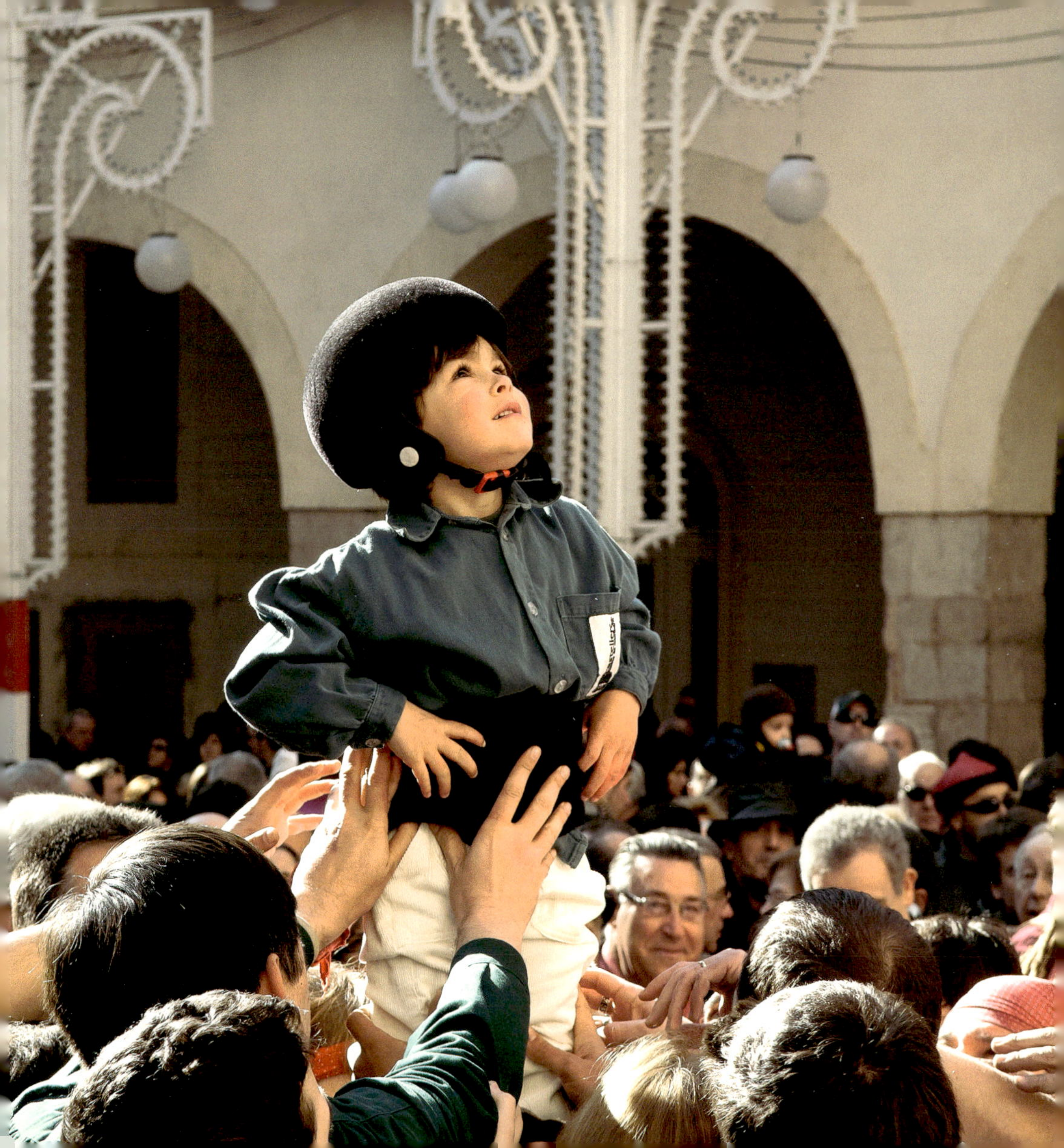

**7.** The *colles*

Colla Vella dels Xiquets de Valls

Colla Joves Xiquets de Valls

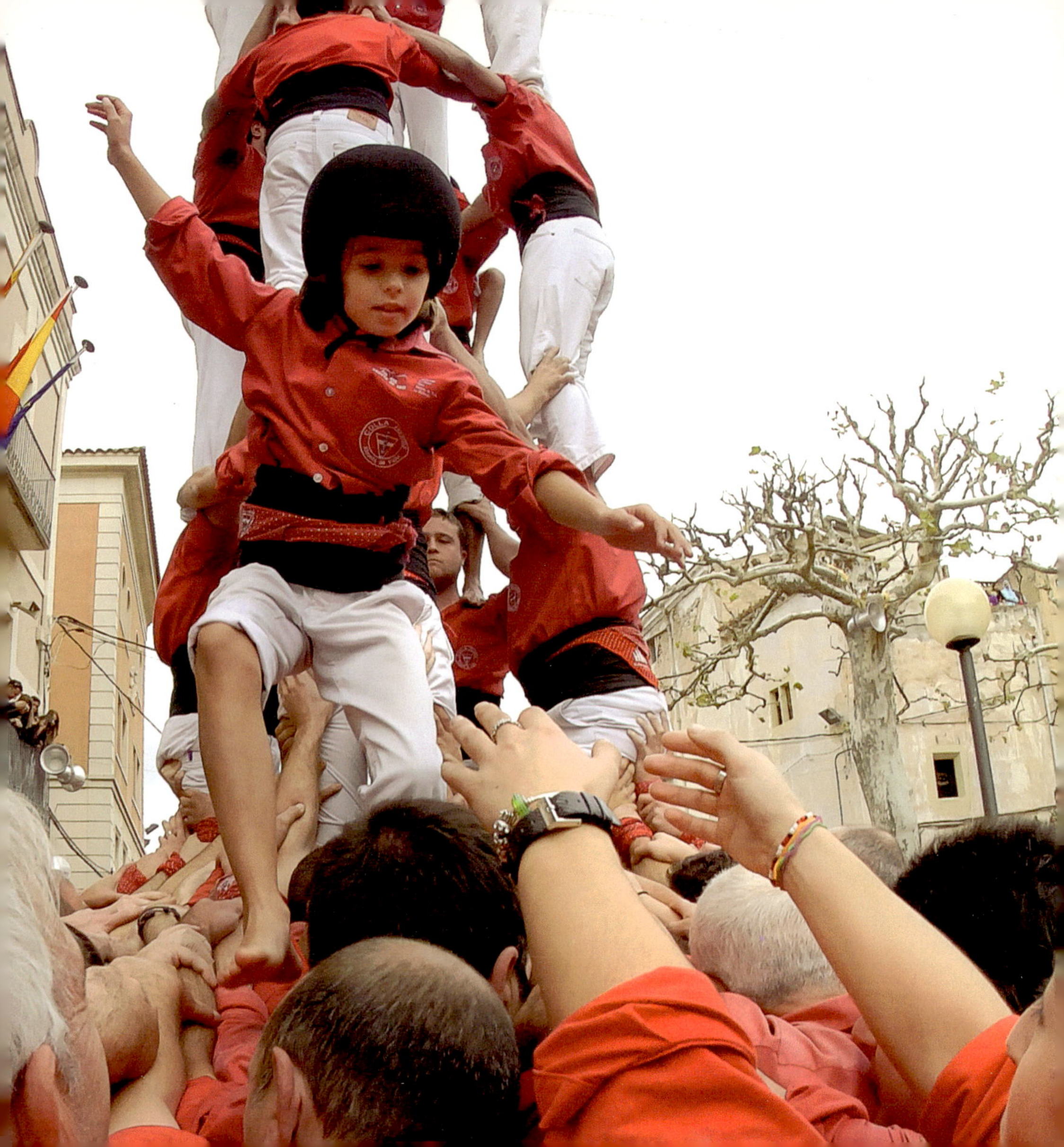

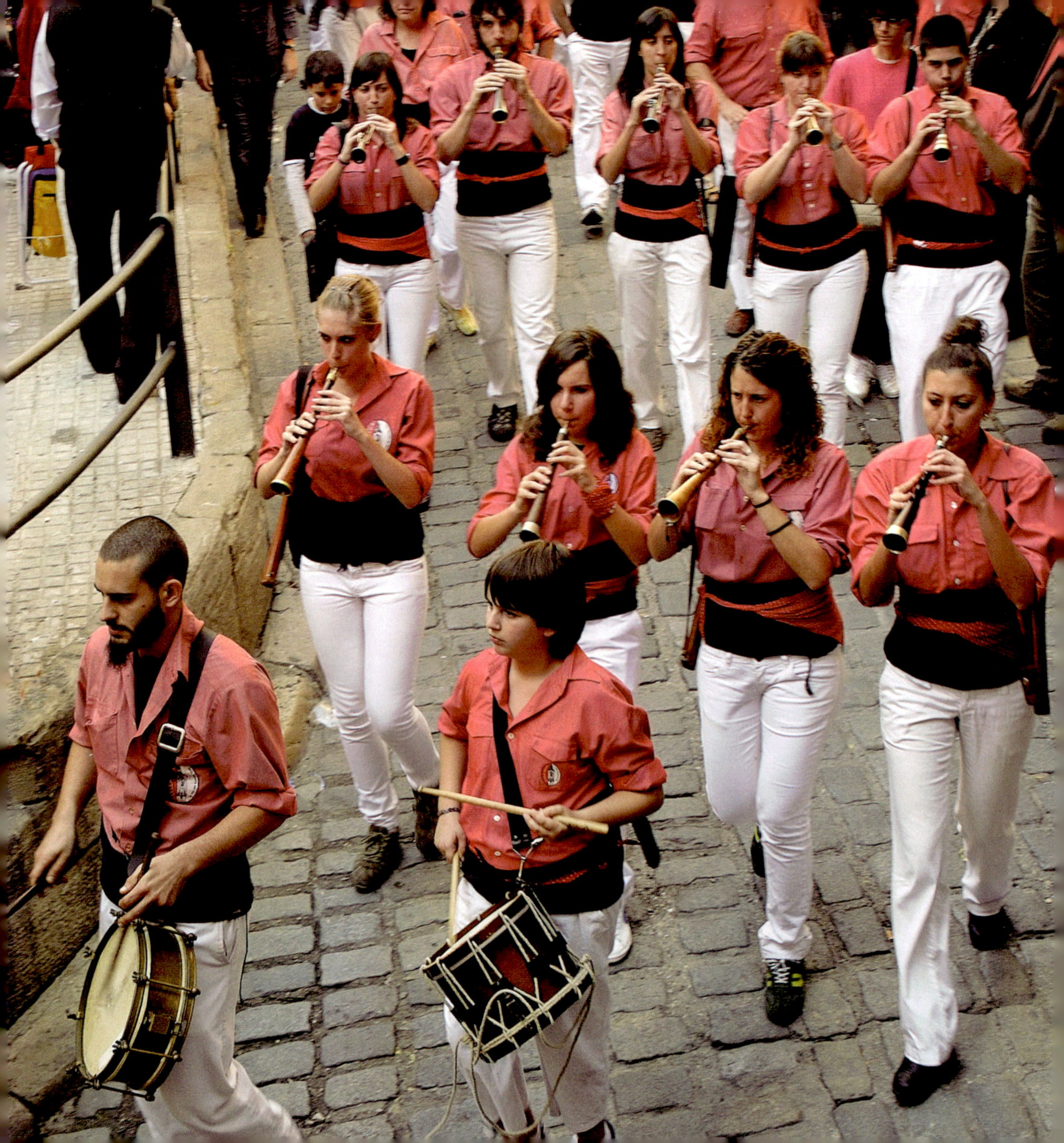

# 8. The music

It almost certainly recalls the origin of the *castells* as part of a dance, but, in no case is it a residual element or without its own function. The music of the *castells*, called *toc de castells* (playing *castells*), is played by at least two *gralles* (shawms) and a *timbal* (drum) and, as we have mentioned, mainly marks the beginning of the construction of the *castell*, the moment when the *enxaneta* does the *aleta*, in other words, when the *castell* is considered built, and its end, once the *castell* has been completed. In the case whereby a *castell* falls, the music stops dead. Generally, the *colles* have their own group of *grallers* and *timbalers*, but some hire out musicians for each event. The tune of playing *castells* has remained the same with few variations over the centuries, although it is also true that many *colles* of musicians have made their own adaptations.

*Grallers* (gralla players) and *timbalers* (drummers) of the Colla Vella dels Xiquets de Valls in formation, followed by the other *castellers* of the *colla*

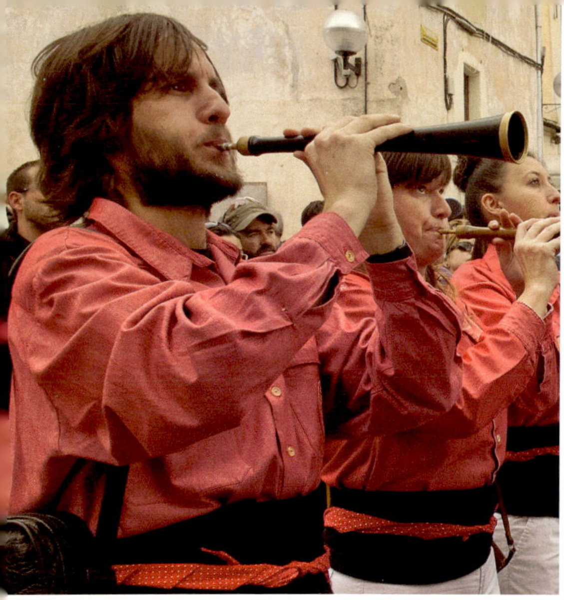

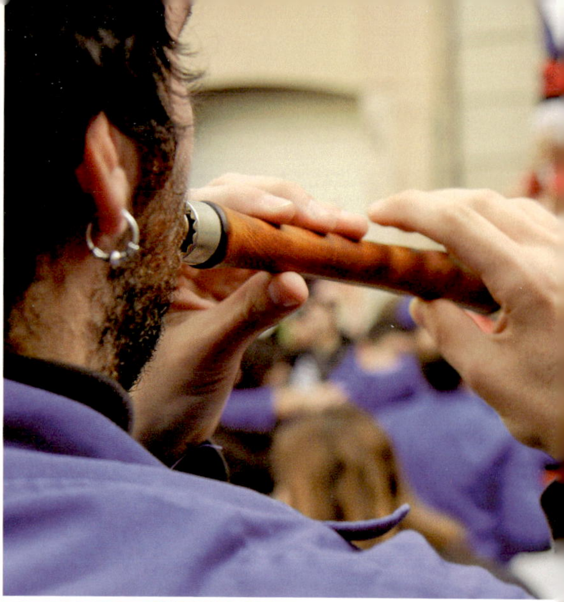

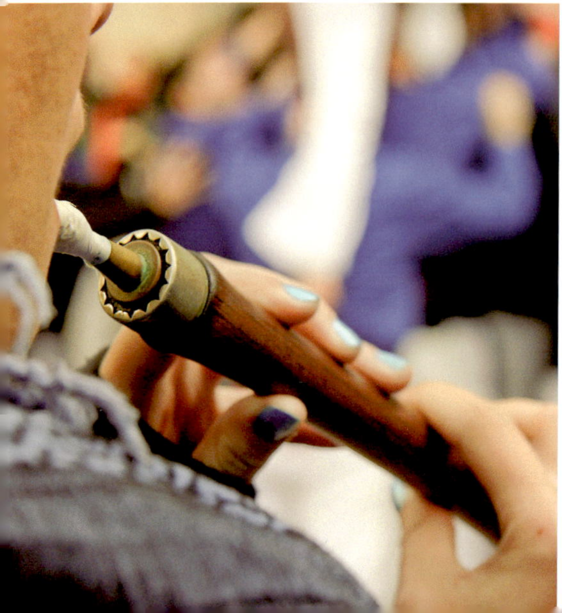

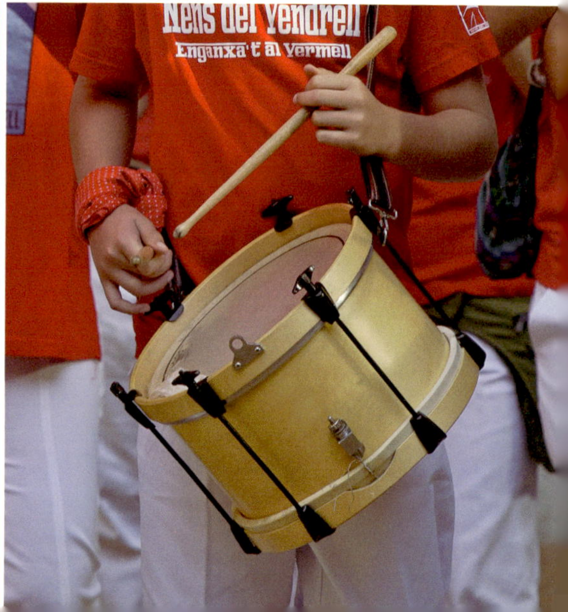
Nens del Vendrell
Enganxa't al Vermell

**8.** The music

Nearly all the *colles* have a group of *grallers* and *timbalers*

**8.** The music

*Grallers* from the Escola de Grallers de Sitges (School)

**8.** The music

Bordegassos de Vilanova

3 of 7 _ You can see the difference of position of the *aixecador* and the *enxaneta* in relation to the current positions

# 9. Two centuries building *castells*

Today, the origin of the *castells* is still a subject of study. It is also true, however, that the most recent work produced by historians has enabled us to rule out, at least, some curious or even outlandish theories about their origins. At this stage, the most accepted explanation about the origins of the *castells* states that, between the 18th and 19th centuries, some small human constructions of a few storeys that formed part of a dance called *Ball de Valencians* (Valencians' dance) caused some rivalry between the groups that did it, and they ended up taking centre stage and their own identity. These small human towers took root in the city of Valls, where they achieved their own character independent of the dance. With gradual changes in the construction technique which enabled them to make them higher and safer, they gradually became something very similar to what we know today as *castells*. At the beginning of the 19th century two *colles* are documented in this city which competed raising the early *castells*, making them higher and more difficult. In Valls, therefore, nearly everyone considers it the birthplace of the *castells*. What is undoubtedly the case is that this city was home to the *colles* that developed the *casteller* activity during the 19th century, and which per-

## 9. Two centuries building *castells*

formed in many of the popular and official festivals organised mainly in the Catalan counties of Camp de Tarragona and Penedès. These *colles* built *castells* of nine storeys even then and reached many of the feats only achieved again a few years ago. But at the end of the 19th century, and due to a notable change in rural society and in the media of the time, the *castells* went into decline and the *casteller* activity was not recovered until well into the 20th century, with the progressive appearance of *colles* outside the city of Valls, and the recovery of forgotten challenges. The construction of the first *castell* of nine storeys in the 20th century by the Colla Vella dels Xiquets de Valls, in 1981, marked the beginning of a new period in the *casteller* world, which brings us to today with, as we have said, some sixty *colles*, and the achievement of higher *castells* and, in some cases, more difficult than those in the 19th century. Moreover, the *castells* and the *colles* that build them have spread all over Catalonia, established themselves in the Balearic Islands, and have begun a promising process of internationalisation.

4 of 8 _ Xiquets de Valls. Vilanova i la Geltrú, 1901

**9.** Two centuries building *castells*

2 of 7 _ Xiquets de Valls. Plaça del Blat, Valls, 1921

2 of 6 _ Xiquets de Valls. 1931. The *aixecador* celebrates the success of the Tower doing the *figuereta*

## 9. Two centuries building *castells*

*Muixeranga* from Algemesí. The *muixeranga* is a dance, almost a series of evocative paintings, that ends up with a human tower. It can be considered an ancestor of the *castells*

**9.** Two centuries building *castells*

*Ball de Valencians* in Tarragona. It is believed that the evolution of the technique of the *Ball de Valencians* to that of the *castells* was gradual, although there were also mould-breaking elements, such as abandoning the other parts of the dance and establishing the same number of *castellers* on each floor of the *tronc*

# Glossary

**aixecador, acotxador or cassoleta** Acording to the *colles*, second storey of the *pom de dalt* and the last but one of the *castell*. It is formed by just one child who, over the *dosos*, covers the *castell* by crouching.

**aleta, fer l' (do the "aleta")** The action or raising the hand that the *enxaneta* does when they crown a *castell*. This action signifies that the *castell* has been *carregat* (built).

**cap de colla (head of "colla")** The person who, generally from the ground, gives exact instructions to the *castellers* to continue building the different *castells*.

**casteller** Each person that makes the *castells*.

**castells (literally, castles)** Human towers that have been in Catalonia for more than two hundred years and which can reach ten storeys in height.

**colla (in plural, colles) (group of friends, team of workers)** Entity or group in which the *castellers* meet. They are usually run through a Committee for administrative tasks and a Technical Committee that is in charge of the rehearsals and deciding the position in the *castell* of each *casteller*.

**diada castellera ("castellera" day)** Performance of one or several *colles* of *castellers* that is usually done to coincide with the local festivals of the town where the performance is made.

**dosos (twos)** First storey of the *pom de dalt* and last but two of the *castell*. They are made up of two children who close the *castell* looking face to face at each other and linking up their arms.

**enxaneta** Third storey of the *pom de dalt* and last one of the *castell*. It is made up of just one child who climbs on top of the *acotxador*. When each of their legs is on either side of the *acotxador* they raise a hand, *fa l'aleta*.

**folre (lining, coating)** A group of *castellers* that in the form of strengthening are placed over the *pinya* and in very difficult *castells* provide solidity to the *castellers* of the second and third storeys.

**llenya, fer (literally, make timber)** In "*casteller*" slang, a *castell* that collapses.

**manilles (rings, bracelets)** A small group of *castellers* who, in extremely difficult *castells*, are placed over the *folre* and act as strengthening to the *castellers* of the third and fourth storeys.

**pinya (literally, cluster)** A group of *castellers*, sometimes hundreds, who form several circles on the ground and who support the base of a *castell*. In Catalan, figuratively, *pinya* is a group of closely linked people and *fer pinya* (make a cluster) refers to cooperating or working together to achieve an objective.

**pom de dalt (pommel or top crowning)** Structure of cupola of three storeys that crowns any type of *castell* except the pillars. The storeys of the *pom de dalt* get the name, from below upwards, of *dosos*, *acotxador* and *enxaneta*. These storeys are always formed by the boys and girls of the *colla*.

**tronc (trunk)** The central structure of the *castell* that begins on the ground, surrounded by the *pinya*, always with the same number of *castellers* by storey, and can be raised by up to seven storeys in height. This structure, on reaching the number of storeys planned, is always crowned with the *pom de dalt*.

© Triangle Postals SL

© Text: **Josep Almirall**

© Photography: **Fèlix Miró:** p. 15, 24, 25, 26, 27, 29, 30, 43, 85, 88, 111, 116b, 117, 119a, 121b, 122a, 134, 135a, 136, 137bc, 145a, 146b, 149, 150ab, 151b, 152b, 158, 160, 163b, 165b, 166b, 167a, 168a, 169a, 175b, 176, 177a, 178b, 179, 181a, 185b, 197b, 198a, 203a. **Xavier Saumell:** 37, 55, 57, 58, 66bd, 68a, 71, 72, 75, 76, 84b, 87, 102, 103, 115, 133, 139b, 140a, 147, 148a, 151a, 159, 161b, 164a, 180b, 185c, 194, 195, 200, 201, 215, 223, 224, 225, 226, 228a, 236, 237. **Carles Castro:** 20, 28, 48, 65a, 79, 84a, 119b, 122b, 135b, 140b, 141a, 145b, 150c, 154, 155, 167b, 168c, 171b, 175a, 177b, 185a, 187b, 204, 205, 211, 221, 231. **Hans Hansen:** 10, 12, 17, 42, 50, 52, 53, 54, 62, 63, 64, 66c, 67, 81, 96, 107, 109, 162b, 187a, 190b, 191a, 199a, 228d. **Ricard Pla:** 8, 21, 23, 36, 39, 40, 74, 101, 123a, 170a, 181c, 183b, 190a, 192c, 193a, 199b, 206, 212. **Eduard Gil:** 14, 19, 56, 65b, 77, 128, 137a, 142, 143, 178a, 182b, 188a, 197a, 207. **Maite Gomà:** 68b, 82, 86, 95, 106, 129, 162a, 168b, 170c, 184, 192a, 210. **Pere Vivas:** 32, 46, 59, 66a, 69, 91, 99, 148b, 172, 173, 191b, 230. **Jordi Puig:** 2, 31, 35, 44, 90, 123b, 209. **Oleguer Farriol:** 16, 60, 73, 105, 161a. **Juanjo Puente:** 51, 121a, 127, 166a. **Emilio García:** 139a, 180a, 188b. **Aina Pla:** 228bc, 229. **Margarida Carrió:** 126, 140c. **Quim Hugas:** 80, 112. **Àngel Closa:** 170b. **Antoni Coll:** 93. **Ferran Quesada:** 34. **Alfons Morillas:** 138c. **Montse Oliva:** 138a. **Lucas Vallecillos:** 4.

CPCPTC: 232. Castellers de Barcelona: 203b. Castellers de Caldes de Montbui: 141c. Castellers de Castelldefels: 153b. Castellers de Cerdanyola: 171a, 193b. Castellers de Cornellà: 183a. Castellers d'Esparraguera: 183c. Castellers d'Esplugues: 182a. Castellers de Mollet: 124b. Castellers del Poble Sec: 182c, 192b, 198b. Castellers del Riberal: 169b. Castellers de Rubí: 171c. Castellers de Sabadell: 163a. Castellers de Sant Cugat: 70, 141b. Castellers de Terrassa: 138b, 165a. Castellers de Vilafranca: 219. Colla Jove Xiquets de Vilafranca: 153c. Colla Vella dels Xiquets de Valls: 146a, 157a, 218, 234, 235. Global de Salou: 124a. Margeners de Guissona: 116a. Matossers de Molins de Rei: 151c. Minyons de Terrassa: 94, 100, 120, 157b, 189. Nois de la Torre: 125, 181b, 193c. Nyeros de la Plana: 153a. Salats de Súria: 152a, 169c. Torraires de Montblanc: 152c. Xiquets de Reus: 139c, 164b.

Original idea: **Marta Prat** and **Josep Almirall**

Agency and management idea: **Martina Ros**

Editorial direction: **Ricard Pla**

Editorial coordination: **Martina Ros**, **Mercè Camerino**

Graphic design: **Joan Colomer**

Layout: **Mercè Camerino**

Illustrations: **Aina Pla Planas**

Translation: **Steve Cedar**

Printed by: **Sanvergráfic**

Registration number: B-12.415-2011
ISBN: 978-84-8478-473-9

Edition subsidised by the Department of Culture and Communication Media of the Generalitat de Catalunya.

Generalitat de Catalunya
Departament de Cultura
**Centre de Promoció de la Cultura Popular i Tradicional Catalana**

With the collaboration of:

**COSTA DAURADA**

AJUNTAMENT DE **TARRAGONA**

**AJUNTAMENT VILAFRANCA DEL PENEDÈS**

COORDINADORA DE COLLES CASTELLERES DE CATALUNYA

Dedication:

To my two daughters, Mireia and Clara, fellow travellers on an infinite number of *diades castelleres*.

*Josep Almirall*

Acknowledgements:

Joan Beumala, Jordi Suriñach, Xavier Brotons, Jordi Castañeda, Guillermo Soler, Joan Borràs, Raquel Sans and, especially, all *colles castelleres*.

# TRIANGLE▾POSTALS

**Triangle Postals SL**
07710 Sant Lluís
Tel. +34 971 15 04 51
www.triangle.cat

No part of this book may be reproduced or used in any form or by any means –including reprography or information storage and retrieval systems– without written permission of the copyright owners. all rights reserved in all countries.